# Complete Guide to Conjuring

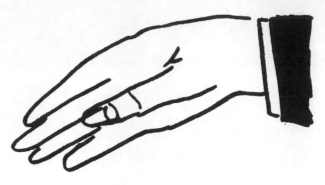

*Also by* Ian Adair:

*Conjuring as a Craft*
*Party Planning and Entertainment*
*Papercrafts*
*The Complete Party Planner*
*Encyclopaedia of Dove Magic* (Vols. 1-4)
*The KnowHow Book of Jokes and Tricks*
*Television Puppet Magic*
*Television Dove Magic*
*Oceans of Notions*
*Magical Menu*
*Magie et tours de passe-passe*

# Complete Guide
# to Conjuring

Ian Adair

Line drawings by the author Photographs, showing the
author's hands in action, taken by A. C. Littlejohns, AMPA

South Brunswick and New York: A. S. Barnes and Company
London: Thomas Yoseloff Ltd

A. S. Barnes and Co., Inc.
Cranbury, New Jersey 08512

Thomas Yoseloff Ltd
Magdalen House
136-148 Tooley Street
London SE1 2TT, England

to
Peter Warlock

**Library of Congress Cataloging in Publication Data**

Adair, Ian.
    Complete guide to conjuring.

    Bibliography: p.
    Includes index.
    1. Conjuring        2. Tricks        I. Title
GV1547.A22              793.8            78-69691
ISBN 0-498-02099-1

*Printed in the United States of America*

# Contents

# Acknowledgments

In thanking the various responsible persons for their kind assistance and contributions in the preparation of this book, I would first like to acknowledge and applaud the brilliance and expertise of fellow Inner Magic Circle member Peter Warlock. Acclaimed as being one of the most knowledgeable magicians of our times, as well as being a prolific magical inventor and writer, he is a true historian; his assistance in preparing the section titled "History of Mystery" is much appreciated.

For his kind assistance in providing my readers with the most up-to-date Glossary of Conjuring Terms ever to be published, my thanks goes to my friend, again a prolific inventor and author, Will Dexter, from England.

Professional commercial photographer Arthur Littlejohns must have taken so many action photographs of my hands, revealing top secrets, that he himself can be in no doubt as to how it is all done. There have not been many of my now sixty books on the subject that he has not been involved in and that have not used his photographic techniques. A special thanks to him for supplying the clear and understandable photographs as used in *Complete Guide to Conjuring.*

Thanks to Bill Milligan, now in Australia, who first accepted me into a local magicians' society even though I was under the age limit; to Robert Harbin, who challenged me to write one-hundred books on the subject; and to English illusionist Jeffery Atkins, who constantly requests me to write and provide more books for the "Adair" section of his gigantic magical library.

My sincere thanks go to all members of the Magic Circle, London, and in particular to president Francis White and secretary John Salisse, who have honored me with their highest award of the gold star for my services to magic, and in particular, for the books I have published.

To William G. Stickland, M.B.E., secretary and past president of the International Brotherhood of Magicians, and to Edwin Hooper, leading magicial dealer in the world, my thanks for inspiration.

# 1  This Is Conjuring

This is conjuring.

Conjuring is a fascinating art, a wonderful hobby, and a lucrative living.

As an art it is parallel with those of painting, music, and drama. The conjurer masterfully uses all three to create his own world of make-believe.

He is an actor playing the part of a conjurer. Not unlike the painter, he is artistic and relies upon art and design for enhancing his act. Like the musician, the tools of the trade, the instruments, in his hands come to life and provide enjoyment for all.

Gone are the vaudeville days, the nights at the music hall, and the extravaganzas that provided family entertainment throughout the world. The masters of magic—Houdini, Blackstone, Chung Ling Soo, Devant, Dante, and others—were truly names to conjure with.

So it is "curtain up" once more. Join me in reminiscing the magic of yesteryear, reviewing the greats as they were in their heyday, delving into the past when the queuing public longed to be baffled and entertained by those great men of mystery.

## HISTORY OF MYSTERY

When primeval man saw the first flash of lightning he saw the magic of the gods, and with the thought of homage to his own particular gods there came man-made magic.

The first attempts were so elementary, but showed a natural cunning that could beguile those of lower mental stature. Those early magicians were the forerunners of the latter-day craftsmen who would make the mysterious entertaining.

Of the pre-Christian era, there is only the sketchiest description of the feats used by the wonder-workers.

The earliest record of a magical performance is to be found in the "Westcar" papyrus, now resting in the East Berlin State Museum. This papyrus, produced approximately a thousand years after the appearance of the Egyptian magician Dedi, before Cheops, the builder of the Great Pyramid (c. 2700 B.C.), tells the story of how this magician supposedly, 110 years old, traveled to the court of Cheops and then: "He knows how to fasten on a head that has been cut off, and he knows how to make a lion walk behind him with his leash on the ground. And he knows the numbers of the secret chambers in the sanctuary of Thoth!" The papyrus is incomplete, but in the translation by Professor Battiscombe Gunn, we read: "Then a goose was brought to him with its head cut off. The goose was placed on the western side of the pillared hall. Then Dedi uttered a magic spell and the goose rose up quivering. And when one had reached the other, the goose stood up cackling. Then he had another goose brought to him and the same was done with it. Then his Majesty had an ox brought to him, its head being cut off, falling to the ground. And then Dedi uttered a magic spell and the bull stood up lowing."

A thousand years lapsed between performance and record, so what really did happen, we can only guess at, for the business of decapitating and restoring is something that seems common to magicians throughout the ages. A good trick, without doubt, and well done!

The oldest trick would appear to that known as the "Cups and Balls" (see page 43), and while there is no mention of Dedi or, for that matter, any other early Egyptian magician performing this trick in the pre-Christian era, it would seem that in many parts of the world, as far apart as Greece and India, forms of this particular piece of deception were being used to entertain and mystify the spectators. In its early form it was usual to have three cups, metal or otherwise, and for a small ball to vanish and then travel to and from the cups into the performer's hands. Today, the trick is a magical classic and is part of the contemporary conjurer's repertoire.

There were other kinds of magic practiced by the priests in the Greek temples. Here, more sophisticated trickery was used, involving ingenious apparatus that could cause a voice to issue from a statue, fire to blaze on command from an earthen vase, and doors that opened at the command of the priest. Such mysteries were, according to the priests, the magic of the gods.

10

Time passes before magic makes its mark as entertainment on the European scene. Only a minority of its population were educated, and to the ignorant, and something most possibly fostered by the priests of those days, there was a fear of witchcraft, and with that fear, the thought that those who could cut and restore a handkerchief could well be in league with the Devil.

Nevertheless, there were many favored, in both England and the Western part of Europe, and the magician, as an entertainer, employing minimal apparatus and a fair proportion of skill, toured the countries in question, performing to crowds surrounding him.

History tells us of Brandon, at the court of Henry the Eighth, and of how he, this master entertainer, one day while in the Royal courtyard, drew the attention of the favored company to a pigeon perched on top of a wall. Taking a piece of chalk, he drew on the lower part, outlining the illustration of a bird. Then taking a dagger in his hand, he struck the center of the outline, and the pigeon suddenly dropped from the wall to be found dead at the courtiers' feet. Such a feat so seemingly magic, and yet performed by simple means, made the king well think that one who could do such to a bird quite equally could do the same to a king, and Brandon was warned to keep such a feat out of his repertoire.

In the sixteenth century there was to be an event that was to help purvey to so many believers what was assumed to be witchcraft.

At Smeeth, a village in the county of Kent, England, there lived one Reginald Scot, a gentleman hop farmer, who not only did much to improve the quality of the hop, but also performed his duties as justice of the peace. One day, before him, at the magistrates' court at Rochester, there appeared a young girl named Margaret Simons, charged with witchcraft. Scot was struck by the cruelty of the prosecution and determined to devote himself to demonstrating the foolishness of popular superstitions about witchcraft and the wonders accomplished seemingly by diabolic influence. For this purpose he set himself the task of understanding a knowledge of the tricks used by entertainers of the day, and in one, a Frenchman named Cautares, he found an excellent teacher. With the knowledge gained of many feats, which, when performed before ignorant people, supernatural means could be the explanation, he put pen to paper and in 1584, his momumental work, *The Discoverie of Witchcraft,* was published in London. Within the 560 pages of the first edition, one chapter, "The Art of Juggling Discovered," deals with the conjuring tricks of the time, and it is of interest to find that the principles used to bring about the effects of those times are still used in contemporary tricks.

With the passing of the Tudors, there came to England the first of the Stuarts, James the Sixth of Scotland, and the First of England, a

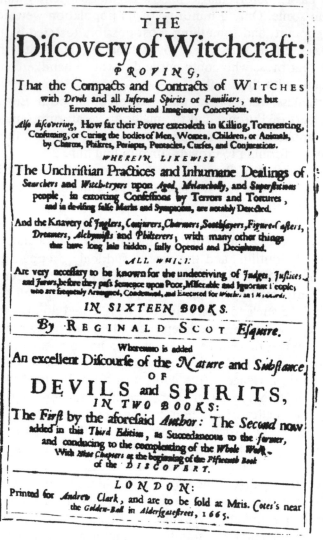

Title page of *Discovery of Witchcraft* (third edition).

man who was fanatical about witches and witchcraft. To him, Scot's
book was anathema and all copies were ordered to be burned. Most
fortunately for students of conjuring, and even more so for collectors
of antiquarian books, many escaped the bonfire, and in recent years, a
fair copy of the first edition has been sold for $3,700.

The coming of the seventeenth century, in Europe in particular,
saw little change in the methods used by the jugglers and conjurers. In
Germany and Holland one hears of Pottage and Ockes Bockes (Hocus
Pocus), and in respect of the term *Hocus Pocus,* there seems evidence to

show that in the early part of that century, an English conjurer used that name.

Playing cards had been introduced, and the conjurer put them to good use, as he did also with the tricks of the Asiatic and Oriental conjurers, among which one using an empty cloth bag, from which several real eggs and a live hen or cockerel were produced, still remains a classic to this day. This trick became a favorite of Fawkes, of whom much has been written. Here was a conjurer who, only commencing his conjuring career at the end of the seventeenth century, came to London, but, with his private soirees, he not only presented the famous egg-bag trick but featured tricks with cards and dice and exhibited a wonderful clock that, when touched by the hand, would play many tunes as well as imitating instruments and bird sounds.

Fawkes, whose exact age is not known, died in 1731, leaving to his widow a fortune at that time.

The eighteenth century was to see the emergence of a larger magical canvas, and for such, one must look to the Italian Giovanni Guiseppe Pinetti. While in the main, the entertainers of the day who specialized in conjuring had performed in the streets, at fairs, or in private rooms, using mostly small-type magic, Pinetti, with magnificent and ornate settings, brought magic to the theater. With his entourage, Pinetti traveled far. In 1784 he was in England featuring an early form of "Second Sight," and breaking the London run for one night to give a Royal Command performance before King George III at Windsor Castle. He traveled to Portugal, Germany, and finally, in 1800, to Russia, where at the comparatively young age of fifty, he was to die.

During his years of performing, Pinetti was to suffer from the many writers who attempted to expose his tricks, these being quite new to the public. Pinetti was a great publicist, always adopting the richest clothes, riding in the best of carriages, and using every means available to exploit his talents. One such trick that has been used by many conjurers since depends on the performer to approach a baker's stall and upon taking a bread roll, and opening it, find a gold piece inside. This would be repeated while crowds gathered round. Whether or not real gold pieces were used and whether as legend has it he distributed them to the assembled company, we shall never know. Most probably the coins used were token disks bearing the name of Pinetti.

Indeed, many were to follow the path initiated by Pinetti, and with the coming of the nineteenth century one hears of Blitz, who, born in Hamburg, Germany, came to England as a small boy, and with the contemporary tricks of the day, added to magic a new dimension, namely that of humor. He was to be welcomed just as much in the United States as in England, and in his book *Fifty Years in the Magic Circle* one gets the impression of his work and the success that attended it.

At this point in time, there were to be heard the accounts of Oriental, Asiatic, and North American magicians, the first two mentioned with tricks that would soon be in the European repertoire, and the last named, with their unusual tent-shaking phenomena.

From the East, already there had arrived a trick that was to become one of the great classics of magic, popularly known as the "Chinese Linking Rings" (see page 59). In this effect, a number of solid metal rings would link and unlink in a truly magical fashion.

One trick that Blitz capitalized on was that where a bullet, loaded into a gun, was fired at the performer, a dangerous trick indeed, and one that has caused many deaths, including that of the famous Chung Ling Soo.

The pattern of Pinetti was to continue with many contemporary performers, among them Philippe and then Anderson, "The Great Wizard of the North," but paradoxically, the complete breakaway was to come from a Viennese civil servant, Joseph Nepomuk Hofzinser. Here was a man certainly a century ahead of his time, introducing his many originations and his new style of magic, which was to be exemplified so many years later by the truly great magicians of our times. Most fortunately, much of his magic has been preserved in written form through the efforts of Ottakar Fischer, and two of his books, *Kartenkuenste* and *Zauberkuenste,* bring to light conjuring that is just as much twentieth century as it was nineteenth. Fortunately, for those unable to read the German language, we owe a debt to Mr. S. H. Sharpe for his translation of *Kartenkuenste,* and the book will soon to be published in Canada, translated by John Gilliland.

In the field of card magic, many feats offered by magicians of today bear the imprint of Hofzinser.

In Europe, apart from Hofzinser, it didn't progress until almost the middle of the century and the days of mechanical conjuring, but a certain change was to come. In France, a young man, a watchmaker of twenty years, had studied, experimented, invented, and perfected a number of conjuring tricks that he felt certain could raise the status of the conjurer. So sure he was that in 1845 he rented a suitable room in the Galerie de Valois in the Palais Royal, and this was converted into a suitable theater for his performances. The name of this conjurer, who can without fear of contradiction, be called "The Father of Modern Magic," was Jean Eugene Robert-Houdin. While the first performance was hardly a success, as is the case with so many first performances, those which followed soon established his supremacy, and he was to continue an active life performing all over Europe for a decade. Unique indeed is the fact that, because of trouble with the natives of Algeria in 1856, the French government persuaded Robert-Houdin to show that his powers of magic were greater than those of the native magicians, and with such feats as the "Bullet Catching" and an illusion of that time called "The Light and Heavy Chest," he succeeded.

His name will never be forgotten, for in his book, *Les Secrets de la Prestidigitation et de la Magie,* though now more than a hundred years old, the stature of his magic is written there for all times.

The half-century mark had come and gone, many of Robert-Houdin's presentations having been copied by other contemporary European conjurers, chief among them Anderson.

A decade was to pass before there was any noticeable change, but one came suddenly, making the efforts of the conjurers of the 1850s completely outdated.

The man responsible for this change was Cheltenham-born John Maskelyne. As was Robert-Houdin, Maskelyne had been apprenticed to the craft of watchmaking, and he, too, had a great interest in conjuring. During a visit to a performance held in Cheltenham Town Hall, of the

John Neville Maskelyne.

15

Davenport Brothers, who professed to be producers of spiritualistic phenomena, Maskelyne probed part of their secret, and he stood up at the conclusion of the performance and loudly announced that not only were the Davenport Brothers frauds, but further, that within a month he would, in the same hall, duplicate, using natural means, the experiments that had been witnessed that afternoon.

Maskelyne kept his word, for using as a partner George Cooke, he and Cooke decided that the presentation of magic could be the profession for them. The year was 1865, and with the exposé of the Davenport seance, plus something quite new, an escape from an examined box, the professional careers of Maskelyne and Cooke commenced with a performance in Jessop's Aviary Gardens in Cheltenham.

A tour of the country followed. The box tricks became part of a sketch, "La Dame et la Gorilla," a trick that later assumed other names, including "Will, the Witch and the Watchman," and was performed under the name of "The Witch, the Sailor and the Enchanted Monkey" by the American illusionist Kellar. It was in 1873 that Maskelyne and Cooke came to London, and after appearing at a few concert halls that they had personally rented, they took over a small hall in the Egyptian Hall in Piccadilly. The hall was rented for a period of only three months, but so successful was this magical combination that both stayed until 1904, when, because of rebuilding of the hall, they had to leave. During this period the British public had seen new life put into magical performances. There had been the birth of the "levitation," some wonderful automata including the whist player, "Psycho," and more than that, the visits of other famous magicians, including famous French magician Buatier de Kolta, inventor of such well-known tricks

**David Devant.**

16

Interior view of St. George's Hall.

as "The Vanishing Lady" and the "Vanishing Birdcage." Above all, there was David Devant, who, with personal charm, stage presence, and his inventiveness, stands out as the greatest magician Great Britain has ever produced. No one who saw him will forget such masterpieces as "The Artist's Dream" or the "Golliwog Ball."

In 1905 the new abode for Maskelyne was St. George's Hall, but Cooke suddenly died and Devant was to become the new partner.

The turn of the century came and passed, and for two decades there was "The Golden Age of Magic." There were many changes; digital dexterity had arrived and with it, artists like the American Thurston and, in particular, Downs, specializing with cards and coins. There, too, was Fowler, "The Watch King," using only watches and clocks, and adding novelty in the variety theaters were the inventors of stage illusions, Servais le Roy, De Kolta, Oswald Williams, Owen Clarke, Walter Jeans, Louis Nokola, and supreme among this elite company, Percy Selbit, who, during his lifetime had no equal in the field of magical invention. In thinking of him, one calls to mind such great feats as "Sawing through a Woman," "The Elastic Lady," "The Human Pincushion," "Through the Eye of a Needle," and "Crushing a Woman."

There were so many big acts. The Oriental extravaganza of Chung Ling Soo, namely Robinson, had such good makeup and publicity that he was thought by the public to be a real Chinese. One feat that was included in his mammoth program was the infamous bullet-catching trick, where, at the Wood Green Empire, London, on the night of

17

**The handcuff king, Houdini. No padlocks, handcuffs, or restraints could keep him from escaping.**

March 23, 1918, it cost him his life, as, in the past, it had killed others. There were so many big acts—Levante in Australia, Dante in America, Roland, Nicola, and one performer, who though a conjurer, made his reputation by escaping from any form of restraint: Harry Houdini. An immigrant from Hungary, he proved through his too-short life to be a master showman. In every country that he visited he proved that there were no handcuffs, leg-irons, bolts, or bars to stop him escaping. His

**A 1909 representation of Houdini at the pinnacle of his fame, by "Nibbs."**

death in 1926, caused by an accidental blow, took from the international magic scene one of its most colorful characters. Ever since his death he has been honored by magicians in the country of his adoption, and as a permanent memorial, there is now a Houdini Museum near Niagara Falls in Ontario, Canada.

These days marked the heyday of variety, but with the Hollywood spectaculars and the opulence of the super cinema, by the thirties, the loyalty of those who had been the mainstays of variety was waning and the death throes of variety were beginning. There was still magic. Cardini, one of the greatest mime-manipulators of all time, continued to lead the procession of good magicians. He had traveled the hard way before there came that worldwide success, from which the innumerable

19

**Cardini, famous manipulator.**

would-be imitators who never reached the magical heights of the original.

The Second World War came, and with it the inevitable demand for entertainment. Such entertainment acted as a lifesaver to all those capable of bringing laughter, joy, and mystification into a troubled world. It was a temporary shot in the arm, but once again the public had the chance to see something new in magic. Making just as big a hit as Cardini had done in the thirties was Channing Pollock with his superb dove act in the fifties, and, just as had been the case with Cardini, imitators sprang up throughout the world. There, too, was the greatest magical extravaganza seen since the days of Chung Ling Soo, presented by Kalanag, with his own magical revue.

There was a bigger demand for a special type of magic, namely that of pseudomentalism, and successes in this field were scored by Dunninger, Chan Canasta, Fogel, Koran, and David Berglas. Today this scene has taken on even greater glamour with the emergence of Uri Geller.

But the days of invention were still with us, and in South African-born Robert Harbin one saw so much that was akin to Selbit. Today the illusions that he personally originates have to be capable of performance surrounded by an audience, which calls for greater ingenuity, and one of his most famous inventions, "The Zig-Zag Girl," must have been seen in every part of the globe.

Holland has been the producer of so many original and clever magicians, supreme among them Fred Kaps. The call for small magic on many occasions has produced outstanding magicians like Albert Goshman, and should many think that magic is the prerogative of the male sex, the distaff side has shown its ability, two of its outstanding representatives being June Merlin of Great Britain and Elizabeth Warlock of Canada.

But in much the same way that once the cinema posed the threat of

Channing Pollock, a remarkable performer with live doves.

Sitta, famous Italian magician and illusionist.

Kalanag, famous German magician, with his full evening show.

Fred Kaps, international Dutch magical personality.

Magicienne extraordinary Elizabeth Warlock from Canada.

competition against the live variety theater, today there is an even stronger competitor in television. Fortunately, the demand for live theater exists, and in the best cabaret nightclub spots the public can enjoy modern magic presented surrounded.

And so today the fascination for magic exists whether presented live or through the television medium.

One must not forget the societies and clubs wherever magicians gather. Of these the oldest and still surviving is the Society of American Magicians, while in Britain The Magic Circle, founded in 1905, is nearly as old. Though a later arrival in the twenties, the largest is the International Brotherhood of Magicians, branches of which have been formed throughout the world.

# 2 How to Be a Conjurer (An Introduction to Conjuring as an Art)

This is more than a book of secrets. It's a wealth of information gathered together from many reliable sources.

It contains the most essential findings one could wish to know about. The subject and material have been designed to inspire ambition, to stimulate the imagination, and to provide the inquiring mind with accurate information told in an interesting style.

It has been written for today's students of magic.

The contents, the reader will find, are well balanced, both in literary and pictorial matter, and are the most attractive, the most accurate, the most readable, and the most stimulating to the imagination.

These are varied and contain new and original magical effects and routines, a great number of which have been specially devised and written for this book.

Here, the backgrounds and workings of the major branches of the art are covered: close-up magic, mental magic, children's entertainment, stage and platform tricks, and illusions. The section detailing some of our classics should be of interest to the student who, wishing to study their secrets, will be able to put them to practice, using them in this modern age.

It is in this chapter that I discuss important factors such as practice and rehearsal, dress, appearance and etiquette, apparatus, misdirection, and publicity matters.

## ADVERTISING AND PUBLICITY

When the student has reached the stage of being able to present a properly formed show, he should be thinking of promoting his talents through the media of press and television.

Brochures, business cards, and personalized stationery are a necessity when negotiating with prospective clients. Such printed items are often the bookers' first impressions, and they should be produced to a high standard.

In preparing a brochure that advertises one's services, one should carefully select the best photographs and illustrations from his collection. In many cases, photographs are specially taken for such brochures, and should the opportunity arise, the student is advised to seek the services of a commercial photographer who can ultimately advise him in what methods these should be taken.

A simple yet striking brochure is one that consists of a single folded sheet, the front adorned with the photograph of the performer, with name and entertainment service alongside. The inside contains advertising copy stating the nature of the entertainment, the services offered, qualifications, address, and telephone number. It is unwise to include fees on such brochures, because these are always fluctuating and, in many cases, vary from venue to venue due to distance and other expenditures.

In providing the student with a typical example of what is required, I am taking the liberty of reproducing sections taken from my own specially produced brochure, designed for bookers of children's entertainment.

### IAN ADAIR

Ian Adair is a professional children's entertainer. He specializes in entertaining children of all ages, including mixed ages and groups and performs under most conditions.

A member of the INNER MAGIC CIRCLE with GOLD STAR, 'The International Brotherhood of Magicians' and honary life member of the 'India-Ring', his services are available to party planners seeking a new and refreshing approach in the entertainment of children.

### PARTIES

Party hats, lots of games and a nice tea help to make it—but have you thought.... .there could be something vital missing.

# CHILDREN'S ENTERTAINMENT BY IAN ADAIR.

## CHILDREN'S BIRTHDAY PARTIES

IAN ADAIR'S super 45 minute programmes of magic, puppets and fun can be presented in *your* home. They can be arranged in hotel rooms, church and town halls and in marquees.

Participation—colorful settings—entertaining presentations.

## FACTORY, SCHOOL, RELIGIOUS and ORGANISATIONS' PARTIES

Party planners seeking entertainment for larger numbers (20 to 2,000 or more) will delight in this particular service.

Whether it be the annual factory party, the Sunday School Christmas Treat, or a function organised by the members of various clubs, IAN ADAIR has the ability to control the situation, providing necessary entertainment for the particular occasion.

His 45 minute shows have been designed to captivate all young audiences and a different programme is ensured for repeat bookings.

## FETES, EXHIBITIONS and OUTDOOR ATTRACTIONS

The wise organiser, planning an outdoor event, should automatically think of the children who will accompany their parents.

A 'Children's tent' or 'room' (admission payable at door, if wished) provides another important attraction.

Caravan holiday camps have featured IAN ADAIR'S performances weekly as a special treat for the children to participate in.

His 45 minute shows work out extremely inexpensive when one considers the quality of the performance and the vast numbers attending.

## TELEVISION—STAGE SHOWS—ADVERTISING

Because IAN ADAIR has appeared on over 200 television programmes, covering BBC, ITV and on American chanels, he has the necessary experience required for the medium. Star appearances on the David Nixon Show, 'Blue Peter' 'Pebble Mill' and in his own weekly TV series 'Magic' (15 minute programmes) with Gus Honeybun, have brought him fame and distinction.

Advertising agencies working for the press and television mediums have constantly used IAN ADAIR'S ideas to promote their products.

Write or phone.
For further details write to. . .
. . . . . . . . . . . . . . . . . . . . . .

27

The back panel of the brochure can be a continuation of the front, using the same colors, and an original line drawing could overlap the front so that part of it appears on the back. Only a small amount of text is required on the back panel, and basically one should outline his entertainment services touching on the venues at which he is capable of appearing.

For example:

IAN ADAIR
_____

Children's Entertainer

available for. . .
birthday and Christmas parties;
school and religious group treats;
factory and works parties;
clubs and organisations' annual children's parties;
caravan and holiday camp entertainments;
television, stage, pantomimes and
advertising promotions.

presenting. . .
   MAGIC. TRICKS. PUPPETS. PAPER TEARING.
COMEDY. . .
with fun and participation well to the fore!

Although letterpress methods are suitable for brochure work, with so many good offset printers in existence, this method has proved both practical and inexpensive, especially if one can supply camera-ready paste-ups. The offset principle eliminates costly line and tone printing blocks and tedious compositing. However, should it be necessary for such offset printers to provide graphic and typesetting origination, it could well be that there will be little saving.

Small, nicely printed business cards are always useful, these being available at all times, ready to submit to potential bookers and to those who seem interested in your service.

Your name, address, and telephone number, together with a brief description of your service or qualifications (i.e., "Children's Entertainer) and possibly an illustration depicting a magical motif are all that are required.

Business cards printed in the thermographic principle on foil and unusual card stocks obviously become distinctive, and the performer has a card that is unique to himself.

Notepaper, headed by your name, address, and telephone number, with a few lines of description detailing the services you offer, plus a line illustration, looks attractive and is just as practical when used to confirm bookings to prospective clients. Personal photographs of oneself are not suitable on notepaper, unless, of course, small quantities are being run. Your face image will change rapidly over the years, and it is unwise to have vast quantities of stationery printed with your photograph.

## Free Publicity

Most performers, amateur and professional, rely on free publicity. Local and national newspapers are always on the lookout for new and refreshing stories of up-and-coming hobbyists, theatrical personalities, and those who have a different story to tell. Local and national television studios look for interesting features in the form of interviews that often include a "demonstration" or go out of their way to present an outdoor film should the material be available.

The student is advised to seek his publicity through the medium of his choice. Remembering that things never do happen on their own, he is suggested to approach press reporters or television news-program editors with an interesting theme or story. The winning of a top magical award, for example, creates interest, and the possibility of the winner taking part in the program, discussing his past experiences and his future, together with a short performance containing one or two of the effects that have brought him distinction, could well be taken up by any enthusiastic editor of a local or national news-feature television show. Such an engagement provides excellent publicity and great prestige for magic as an art, plus the fact that an additional income in the form of a fee would be forthcoming to the participant involved.

## Paid Advertisements

Keeping one's name in front of potential clients is a necessity for all tradesmen, the magician included. Daily and weekly newspapers carry classified advertisement sections, covering all entries of professions. For as little as two dollars a week, your services can be recorded under the banner of "Entertainment." Here's an example:

Super 45-minute programs featuring MAGIC, PUPPETS, and FUN, suitable for all age groups. Parents, make YOUR child's party a special one and relax while your young guests are in the capable hands of IAN ADAIR.
Or for a more sophisticated offering:
The immaculate IAN ADAIR presents his slick, sophisticated act (30-45 minutes) as seen on BBC and ITV programs "Pebble Mill,"

"Blue Peter," and "The David Nixon Show." Mystery, suspense, comedy, and participation.

In preparing copy for a displayed advertisement, first be sure that your ad warrants such a coverage. Space ultimately costs money, and should the service not warrant the space that you have selected, you are literally throwing money away.

### Advertising in Other Ways

By advertising one's services in the Yellow Pages of the telephone directory, the advertiser can yet publicize his name so that the many readers will use it for further reference. With so many trade entries, all listed under their individual sections, more and more people are referring to this form of advertising to satisfy their needs when a particular requirement or service has to be considered. A small panel advertising your service can appear in the Yellow Pages of the telephone directory for the minimum of one year. During this period, potential bookers will refer to the section labeled "Entertainments or Entertainers," and should your advertisement attract their attention, business will flourish. One should never include fees or prices in such ads. If you happen to provide an excellent service, one that covers a wide area and is competitive pricewise, mention such things in the space provided. Should your service be an inexpensive one, use words such as *reasonable* or *extremely competitive* rather than *cheapest in town* or *lowest charges anywhere.*

Local television companies provide opportunities for the entertainer to advertise, these usually consisting of a series of spots, reasonably priced considering the numbers viewing.

The ten-second appearances provide enough time for the lazy newspaper or magazine reader to take note and remember the specialized service you have to offer.
Here is an example:

Still caption. . .
Depicts a magical motif on one side while bold print displays your name and address.

IAN ADAIR
The versatile magician.
Children's parties. Sophisticated shows. Outdoor Attractions.

Phone . . . . . . . . . . . . . . . Address . . . . . . . . . . . . . . . .
Make your event a memorable one. Engage a professional!

While the illustrated caption (normally provided by the studio) is shown on screen, a somewhat different dialogue is spoken in the background.

Here is an example:

> The children's favorite entertainer. Obtainable for birthday and Christmas parties, school and religious groups, factory and works parties. Clubs and organizations' annual parties, caravan holiday camp entertainments, motor shows, exhibitions, stage and advertising promotions.

> Publicity giveaways in the form of diplomas, printed balloons, and personalized pencils, advertising your name and profession, are further advertising aids.

> Offset reproduction photographs of the performer for distribution are always welcomed by fans and by those who engage you.

> Specially printed badges, those depicting a magical motif with the performer's name alongside, greatly assist in publicizing a children's show, where children actually wear the badge concerned. Word-of-mouth recommendations are far the best when one is seeking further engagements.

## CHILDREN'S MAGIC

By far the most lucrative of all branches of the art, especially to the semiprofessional performer, is the entertainment of magic to children, at birthday and Christmas parties, factory and works' annual events, in children's tents, at outdoor attractions, and on stage at holiday camps and schools.

There are birthdays galore each day, and in growing up, the child is given numerous parties by his or her parents over a certain period of time. I know of one performer who presents seven different forty-five-minute shows per day, at various venues, at a charge of approximately fifty dollars a show. He's a professional, of course, but like so many, started some years ago as an amateur performing a few bits and pieces at family birthday parties. He has since studied the art of controlling children and carefully selecting the right material for their entertainment, and he has injected his own personality into his show. He is *different*—an entertainer with a new approach.

The beginner will soon realize that entertaining children can be a tiring but pleasurable experience. New and different shows to devise and prepare, traveling to homes and venues, and coping with all types of children, young and old, are but a few of the pleasures one can encounter.

31

Unlike adults, who expect sophisticated conjuring, children expect to see bright and colorful magic of the type that displays bold and attractive-looking properties. They, in fact, prefer story-type magic, with "sucker" climaxes, and adore pretty tricks rather than complicated sleight-of-hand or involved card tricks. They prefer to be *entertained* rather than be fooled. The performer has to be a comedian of a sort, a bit of a fool, and be able to let his hair down without embarrassment to himself. The "stiff" approach using recited patter lines is outdated as far as methods go today.

A magic show designed for children should, in my opinion, not exceed one hour, forty-five minutes being more appropriate. It has been found through experience that time allows the performer to introduce a varied selection of tricks performed at a steady pace. Some performers work extremely fast, romping through trick after trick, while others have a softer but still humorous approach at a slower pace. Whichever style the performer delivers, it is unwise for him to bore his young audience by presenting "time wasters," solely to lengthen his program.

Standard conjuring tricks, given a different approach, can, with suitable patter and routine changes, be used in the children's program.

Magical apparatus, designed solely for the children's show and manufactured ready to use, is available from most magical dealers. Here, properties made in wood, metal, cloth, and various other materials have been made to appeal to the child's imagination. Cutout figures of well-known cartoon characters play a vital role in such a show, for the children recognize these immediately without prompting. Try using nursery rhyme tricks and those which *contradict* themselves (i.e., "Boys and girls, here's a photo of my little *black* rabbit. . .what!. . .it's *white*. . .no, it's *black*. And here's another picture of my little *white* rabbit. . .what! . . . it's *black*, you say. . .*black*. Well, that's funny, for they must have magically changed places, for here on this side is my little *black* rabbit and over here is my *white* one. Aren't these clever rabbits?. . . Let's give them applause!"

This particular trick is that of a transposition of one rabbit card for another, but it has the scope for the entertainer to introduce byplay and "business." It has a sucker climax, the sudden change. Although the performer appears to be 'silly' at first, he ultimately fools them in the end. He has entertained them, in fact, and that's the purpose of his vocation. So that every child is involved, the performer can say, "We all helped to make the rabbits change places by using the magic spell . . . let's all applaud!," thus really obtaining applause for himself. I once overheard the conversation of an adult who, after viewing my children's show from the back of a crowded hall, said, "He's wonderful; the children kept on applauding." She was right, the children did applaud, but more than once I had already *asked* the children to show their appreciation by putting their hands together.

The stage settings and tables that the children's entertainer uses should be colorful, attractive, and impressive in appearance, as well as being practical for transporting. The majority of tables available are suitably designed with various magical themes and motifs, such as colorful cutouts of rabbits and clowns, and all fold flat for packing. Some cleat together, while others simply slot in place. Rear struts pivot out to stand fronts upright while tops hook into position. Some of the stronger-type tables fit together by nuts and bolts, while a great many consist of tubular shafts in plated aluminum with thin, draped tops sometimes adorning hanging banners. The music-stand table with deep, clothed top should be avoided. Rather old-fashioned in appearance and unsturdy for most occasions, it has been succeeded by more modern designs.

Awkward, backward, and disabled children must be treated most carefully, should the occasion arise when such children may form part or all of your audience. It is all very nice to "tick off" a "smart child," the type who tries so hard to spoil the show for the others, but in front of an entire audience, it is hardly the place to do it. Controlling children of all ages, races, and creeds can, and in many instances will be, a difficult problem when one first embarks into the field of children's entertainment. The professional finds, through trial and error, that every child can be dealt with rationally and strictly without being made a spectacle of. Performers who occasionally use whistles, bells, and constantly shout "Quiet" are not true children's entertainers and should never be faced by any audience.

The performer who wishes to select children to assist him in his presentation should first study child psychology. One will find shy children, brash children, downright rude children, nice children, aggressive children, and vulgar children; the list is endless, and you can be assured that at most shows a certain amount of such types will be prominent. One professional, noticing from the start that one particular boy was about to become trouble, made him assist in the earlier part of his show. The magician controlled him admirably by making him part of the performance. Another child, a rather loud, talkative girl, was asked to stand up and help the magician: "I would like you to personally guard the house, or shall we say, the Palace," said the performer, smiling. "Go toward the door, open it, and stand outside . . . that's it. Now close it ever so carefully so that you will be in charge of this party." The child, now contented to rule, does not know, in fact, that she is being rejected and is no longer a part of the show, which can now continue uninterrupted. Of course, this is a last resort,

33

and I advise the method only to be used in cases where a particular child has been unmanageable and is misbehaving so as to spoil the show for all.

The performer is advised to select a well-varied program, avoiding similar effects and limiting the "sucker"-type tricks to a minimum. He should study and learn the routines, movements, and patter lines by heart, planning where unwanted articles should be discarded when preparing a clean surface on the table for others to be displayed upon. A colorful box, one made in a stout cardboard, can be made to fold flat, at the same time being able to be erected in a matter of seconds, assisting the performer in discarding unwanted properties. My own box boldly displays the words "Box of Magic," and I make the point of taking items from it as well as discarding these when the tricks are over. It is a dual-purpose receptacle.

Commence your show with a breezy opener, an effect that can be performed quickly and that will definitely register with the audience.

Hello boys and girls . . . what a lovely party this is and it's a very special one too, a birthday in fact . . . isn't it? [emphasizing the fact that the children are lucky to be attending the party and really thanking the parents of the birthday child, who appreciate this subtle, yet planned mention.] I'm a magician, and do you know, I have been asked to come along to this lovely party to entertain you all with my magic. First, I must tell you that every magician must learn three important things. The magic spell . . . every magician has his own magic spell . . . does anyone here know a magic spell? Hands up those boys and girls who know a magic spell. [Several, if not all, raise their hands.] Yes . . . [pointing to a child] what is your magic spell? [ The children shout out names like "Abracadabra," "Hokus Pokus," "Hey Presto," "Sim Sala Bim," and many others, some of which they make up themselves, adding more fun to the routine.] Well, mine is simply "Abracadabra" . . . shall we try it? All together! On the count of three, I want you all to shout out the magic spell. One . . . two . . . THREE! ABRACADABRA! That's it. . . . very good. The second important thing is "magic blowing." I use magic blowing in a lot of my tricks. Fill your cheeks with air, like this [do so by puffing your cheeks]. Ready . . . one . . . two . . . .THREE blow! . . . that's it! And last, but not least, the magic wand. Every real magician has a magic wand and I have got mine here today. Would you like to see it? Here it is [display wand] and let me say, it's a very clever magic wand, for I intend waving it over all you boys and girls so you will vanish from sight . . . well, I didn't really mean that. Let's use it to help the magic work in the tricks I have brought along today.

This opening routine may, at first, appear cold in print, but I can assure you of the reaction. It's the ideal opening for any children's show, whether large or small. No matter the numbers attending or the venue or function of which they are guests, the routine stays unchanged, and I have found that there is always a certain amount of ad-libbing when answering your magic-spell questions. In fact, no two children's shows are ever the same, even though they consist of identical material. Shows planned for one age group seem to go better than those designed for a mixed one. The reason is simple. Material designed for three-year-olds and presented in a show of mixed ages cannot possibly interest the children who are coming into their teens.

Entertaining children, although sometimes being a thankless task, does have its rewarding moments. One receives the great pleasure of seeing the young audience enjoy themselves, somewhat entering into a world of make-believe.

Children's entertainment as a service is live, topical, colorful, and mysterious. It is exciting, unpretentious, bewildering, and rewarding.

Children love magicians, and magicians love children. Without them where would the children's entertainer possibly be?

## DRESS, APPEARANCE, AND ETIQUETTE

The amateur performer invariably overlooks important aspects such as dress and appearance when planning his act. More often than not he diverts his attention toward the tricks that will form his program, not giving careful and proper thought and consideration to the clothes and makeup he intends wearing.

Sadly, the traditional magician's dress—evening tails, cloak, white gloves, and cane—are not worn as much as they were in vaudeville and music-hall days. Such immaculate dress conjured up a mysterious picture of the real magician in all his glory.

In place, more modern styles and colors are being worn, some especially designed for the performer by theatrical costumers: jackets and waistcoats made from glimmering Lurex, suits in deep velvets or smooth mohair, and zip-up cat-suits with no pockets or fly fronts.

The magician's female assistant should also be dressed to a high and professional standard. From long and slender evening gowns made from the best of materials, to the scantiest of briefs and fish-net tights, she plays a vital role in such a double act where misdirection and appearance are important factors.

However, unless the beginner can afford to spend substantial sums on these luxuries, which many professionals class as essentials, he is best advised to use sensible clothes from his personal wardrobe. Should he not own the latest in evening wear, a smart and modern lounge suit will suffice, suiting the purpose and occasion admirably. Certainly, a fashionable bow tie and matching pocket handkerchief assist in improving his appearance.

A clean shirt, neatly laundered, and a pair of well-polished shoes are two further pieces of dress the performer should carefully look after, for every detail of his appearance is scanned, examined closely, and ultimately criticized by his demanding audience.

If the student is fully confident that his dress and appearance are to his liking, he will be halfway there to becoming a better and more knowledgeable performer.

Hair should be smartly groomed, hands spotlessly clean, paying particular attention to the fingernails, which should always be neatly trimmed. Remember, the magician's hands are always under close observation!

### Make-up

Most amateurs, both in dramatics and in general entertainment, like to feel theatrical, and making up becomes part of the fun.

However, makeup should only be used and applied when and if necessary. Unfortunately, many amateurs use the special cosmetics solely to "feel theatrical," when in fact these are not really required. Often, one cannot help but smile at the male who is heavily made up, when, applied with wrong, or too much, makeup so that he looks appalling and somewhat feminine.

Here are a number of tips in regard to applying makeup.

1. First, determine if makeup is really necessary.

2. Should the performer be appearing under strong lights with spotlights or floods in use, makeup is an additional advantage. When applied correctly, makeup counteracts the effect of strong lights and should present the performer as much like his natural self, as if the lights were not there.

3. Under strong lights on stage, compare the difference between the actual performer who has been correctly made up to the spectator who has suddenly been asked to come forward and appear by your side. The performer appears to be handsome and clean, while the assistant looks pale, somewhat ill, and often dirty.

4. In effect, the aim of applying makeup is to exaggerate the natural color and features of the skin and not to add markings that are not necessary.

5. Since there are two types of makeup—straight and character—it is intended here to detail the basic requirements for "standard" makeup,

because this more than likely applies to the majority of readers.

Set yourself before a well-lighted mirror.

Should you be performing in a well-lighted dining room or club room, a basic appliance is to dip a powder puff into flesh-colored powder, tapping it all over the face, discarding unwanted surplus with the opposite side of the puff. The resulting effect is that any apparent shine, appearing while under hot and fairly bright lights, or in an overheated room, is suddenly dulled and softened. Most drug stores and department stores sell a complete range in the form of compacts of solid powder block. These often come complete with an application pad, being offered in a wide selection of colors and shades. It has been found, though, especially among male performers, that "Suntan" is the shade best suited for the skin.

For concert and stage work, club and cabaret conditions, those which are powerfully lighted, the following makeup methods and cosmetics in general should be purchased and carried in a case used solely for this purpose.

> One stick no. 5 greasepaint
> One stick no. 9 greasepaint
> One stick no. 2 or 3 carmine
> Box or tub of flesh-colored powder
> A good powder puff.
> A black liner
> An orange stick
> One tin of greasepaint remover
> One or more towels

### Applying the Makeup

Placing a towel around the neck, apply a small quantity of grease to the face. Rubbed in well by the fingers, this is wiped off with a towel. With number 5 stick, apply in strokes, onto the forehead and on both sides of the cheek. A stroke over the nose and one on the chin completes what can be accepted as the first applications.

The makeup is spread evenly over the face by the fingertips, which massage the substance into the skin, and is applied similarly to the chin and neck.

## THE MAGICIAN'S APPARATUS

An essential part of the magician's act is his equipment. Whether these be small pieces for close-up work or more elaborate stage properties and illusions, they must be carefully selected.

A poor piece of apparatus is best left out of the act, for it could never give its owner the confidence he requires. The difference between a few extra dollars in the making or buying of better properties can result in a more professional-looking stage presentation.

The beginner should, therefore, study the various magical effects that are advertised in magical dealer's catalogues. These people know their job well, many having been in business for most of their lives. They are willing to assist in all matters concerning possible sales of theatrical equipment for the practicing magician, and the majority issue lists, fliers, and catalogs periodically. While some operate retail shops in cities, others specialize in mail order, providing a fast delivery of their goods to most parts of the world.

The few magicians' magazines that are published also provide a source of information on the magical scene today and carry numerous advertisements of leading manufacturers and suppliers.

Tricks, large and small, invariably carry detailed instructions right down to the suggested patter lines one could use while presenting the effect. Manufactured items range from anything between one dollar upward to several thousand dollars, and should a magician require a "special" from one of the firms who specialize in making "one offs," he can expect to pay considerably more.

When buying from a magical dealer, it must be understood that you are also purchasing and receiving a secret. Often, the cost of the item includes the price of a secret, and in several cases the apparatus is merely there to accompany the detailed instruction sheets. Many prototypes and improved versions, all costing time and money to the dealer, have to be considered in the pricing of an item. There is the inventor to think about, the man who has the brainstorm in the first place. Often a pet trick from a leading magician or inventor becomes an exclusive in a dealer's catalogue, the contributor being either offered a certain amount of money or a credit note that enables him to purchase supplies of magical apparatus for his own act.

In selecting magical apparatus from dealer's catalogs and fliers, the beginner should consider these points:

Although all advertised effects are practical in working and have a potential entertainment value, not all will suit the purchaser. Even after buying a trick, which at first was appealing, the beginner often finds that he has chosen unwisely, selecting an item that requires much dexterity when in fact he really wanted a self-working miracle. Many catalog advertisements emphasize such points in phrases such as "Easy to do," "Self-working," "For the magician who already knows the techniques."

However, a trick that seems impossible to perform in the beginner's hands can and has been presented successfully by more competent magicians, proving that it is not the tools of the trade alone that make one a performer, but the method in which one handles them.

Purchasing the finest piano in the world does not necessarily mean that the buyer will be a more competent pianist. In the same sense, the latest electronic kitchen gadgets enabling the housewife to speed up standard procedures at home may not improve the cooking.

So, the beginner, having decided which branch of the craft he aims to be involved in and then selecting the apparatus that is suited to his style and pocket, is being decisive.

"Piracy," the copying of other magician's personal effects, should always be avoided, although quite a number of magicians still indulge in this unfair practice. Often is the case where the magician usually tries to emulate the effects and styles of others who are prominent in their profession, presenting somewhat similar effects, but presenting them badly. The beginner, therefore, should avoid becoming a carbon copy of those who have devised their own tricks and routines.

Magicians invariably overlook the old magical effects and principles, more often than not seeking something new. That which is classed as being old to one section of the public is new to another. The classic effects, for example, are new and alive to our modern-day audiences. After all, today's public was not around when these classics were originally conceived and put to practice. Although modern techniques and equipment have assisted the magician in forming original themes, the classics remain the best.

Magicial apparatus made in wood, metal, plastic, or cloth materials should be attractive in appearance, practical in working, and adaptable to the performer's needs.

If a manufactured item is highly priced, this need not mean that it is more effective in performance. In reverse, smaller and more common-place materials, such as bottle tops, pieces of string, paper clips, and playing cards, have proved to be more acceptable to an audience that is familiar with household items such as these.

Not all apparatus has to be purchased. This book alone contains the secrets and workings of numerous magicial effects. Most have been specially devised for the reader to make and develop and are, therefore, not otherwise available.

If you are a craftsman in wood, metal, or plastics, you will be competent in manufacturing your own equipment to your own standards. Should you be incapable of manufacturing in any material, I strongly advise you to leave the making to the experts, while you learn the tricks of the trade, the presentation, and the ability to put over the tricks that are to be used.

# MISDIRECTION

Misdirection plays a vital part in the presentation and working of magical effects. While the performer diverts his audience's attention toward another area or hand, he executes the secret move. This action is called *misdirection,* and in many cases magicians use their glamourous assistants to bring about the same results.

In close-up magic, misdirection enables the performer to present more effective sleight-of-hand. The photographs as shown in the close-up sleight-of-hand chapter of this book are good examples, displaying misdirection to its fullness.

For example, in placing a ball into the open left hand, when in fact it has been secretly stolen away by the right, and in closing the supposedly filled fist, displaying this high, the eyes of the spectators will invariably follow the movement to its climax. Meanwhile the right hand, palming the "stolen" item, "ditches" it elsewhere. Misdirection has assisted the performer in creating another close-up miracle!

The performer who introduces an attractive assistant in his act uses misdirection in a different manner. Such assistants generally enter, are handed various unwanted objects, and then finally exit. Some actually are involved in the workings and presentation of the tricks. It is during such entrances and exits of assistants that the performer cleverly introduces his misdirection. Spectators are suddenly distracted by the movements and appearance of the assistant so that the performer can cheekily prepare maneuvers that are quite unseen to his audience.

Pickpocketers use misdirection to enhance their particular line of business.

In mentalism and in "spoon-bending" experiments, such as those presented successfully by Uri Geller, misdirection has always seemed to play the major part in producing the effect. While one of the keys or spoons was prominently displayed in one hand, another, held in the second, was secretly bent. It is only later that the audience realizes that the spoon or key that did not react at that time does so after the time misdirection is introduced. The audience is never really aware of which spoon or key is intended to bend, for the performer himself gives that impression. For example, a ring worn on the finger, there to be seen and admired, can assist the performer tremendously in this experiment. With several keys being offered, two are held in the right hand, while one is displayed in the left. The fact is that the single key can be cleverly engaged into the inside rim of the ring, where it can be levered. It bends! While the performer displays both or several keys in his hands, he emphasizes the fact that only *one* of these *may* bend. The fact is that the key that is inserted into the rim of the ring bends, and it does this quickly, thus resulting in the perfect key-bending stunt of the century. These are my own personal views on how such experiments as these could possibly be executed.

Misdirection assists the magician in a great many tricks and illusions. Used wisely, it uplifts the standards of magic.

## PRACTICE AND REHEARSAL

Whether it be an impromptu offering or a full-scale platform show, the performer must, at all times, practice the various stages of his act. The planning and arrangement of each trick and routine invariably take considerable time to evolve, and the student should aim for a professional outlook. The audience will be aware of such professionalism.

The performer's timing, his appearance, and the content value of his act can only be derived through constant and laborious practice.

Unfortunately, most beginners are faced with unforeseen problems that they did not encounter at first. A patter line that does not register, for example, could put a good performer off his balance, losing complete control of both himself and his audience. It is only by performing constantly and under various conditions that the student can gain confidence in both himself and the tricks he intends performing. An extremely good performer, using adequate material, may not score heavily, lacking general show-business talent or not being able to deliver the performance as it should appear professionally.

The average magician places too much emphasis on the content material of his show than on the entertainment potential, which should always be at the back of his mind at all times.

Here are definite points of information that should be valuable to the beginner as well as to the advanced performer:

Practice each trick separately until the working and routine are perfect. Avoid unnecessary movements and strive to make the actions clear and simple. Display items elegantly, introducing flourishes, which not only enhance the presentation but assist in the handling of the tricks. Practice in taking a bow, showing someone to his seat, walking on and off stage and general stagecraft. There are tricks of the trade in every craft!

Practice in front of a mirror, and should a musical background be required, work to a record of your choice. Try to avoid using loud and brash tunes, such as those offered by the many rock groups and pop singers. Soft, breezy, lilting tunes are by far the best and, the performer will find, easier to work to.

Learn how to ask for applause. At the climax of a trick, work up to the point where the audience realizes that it is over and open your arms out wide while saying "Thank you." Your applause will follow.

After you have practiced each trick, form your act. Design this so that each trick blends into one another and so that no repetition is there. A complete act of producing silk handkerchiefs from a box, although being a clever one, would unlikely succeed, because of the repetition.

Learning the tricks and working them before a mirror are a good start, but performing them live, before an audience, is another.

Like conditions, audiences differ tremendously.

The student should learn how to control an audience, deal with any hecklers or unforeseen difficulties, and realize whether or not he is registering.

As in most things, it is the presentation that counts.

A bunch of flowers stuffed into a paper sack would far better be presented as a beautiful bouquet with paper, foils, ribbons, and cellophane trimmings. It's presentation: the same goods—but presented in an appealing fashion.

So, the student must practice his act to suit his style and under the conditions in which he intends working. As he presents his show he should take special interest in the way in which his audiences are reacting.

It is not how many tricks you can do, but how many you can do well!

# 3 Conjuring Classics

Here is the great magic of the past, recaptured step by step with illustrations to assist the student in presenting what can be called the greatest tricks of our times.

The famous "Chinese Linking Rings," for example, a classic if ever there was one, and the "Egg Bag," made famous by the Great Levante, are but two of the numerous classics offered in this chapter.

The ancient "Cups and Balls," with its original methods and principles, has been given an up-to-date presentation so that it can be performed close up, anywhere, anytime.

"The Multiplying Billiard Balls," a complete routined sequence, in fact, and methods of using the magician's favorite unseen gimmick, the "Thumb Tip," form part of this classical collection.

The proverbial rabbit from the hat is described, too, and providing the student has a top hat and rabbit, the feat can still be accomplished just as it was so many years ago.

"Super Sponges" and a simple version of the clever "Four Ace Trick" complete what I feel are the essential classics one should know about.

Even today, many professional magicians use these tricks in their commercial programs, proving that the classics are just as alive today as they were when they were first introduced.

## THE FAMOUS CUPS AND BALLS

In this, the most beautiful of tricks, the magician performs sleight-of-hand at its very best. Here, with the aid of three goblets and one small ball, the audience witnesses numerous productions, vanishes, reproductions, transformations, penetrations, and, in fact, a complete series of most unbelievable happenings right under its nose, for "Cups and Balls," although on occasion performed as a platform item, is more than suited for close-up work where people surround the conjurer.

The cups I use in my own program were specially made by the late Burtini, a fine English craftsman and producer of precision-made products for the magical profession. The fact is that, although these are unfaked, they are correctly made for presenting the famous trick, and before obtaining a set the student is advised to practice the routine using clear tumblers, watching every move closely through the plastic or glass.

I have viewed superb presentations where the performer has used common plastic or polyethylene beakers, these being practical, if not elegant.

### The Apparatus Required

> Three goblets or plastic opaque beakers
> Four small sponge or cork balls
> Three large sponge balls
> A magic wand (obtainable from
> magical suppliers or made from
> a fourteen-inch length of wooden
> dowel, painted black with two white
> tips, one at each end).

### The Set-up

The three large balls are hidden within the right trouser pocket.

Three of the small balls are held in the left trouser pocket.

The fourth ball is placed within the bottom cup, with the remaining two nested on top.

The entire set should be displayed as follows.

The nesting cups should stand upright, mouths upward to the left of your working area. The magic wand should be nearby, easily accessible.

### The Routine

Display the cups. Pick them up in your left hand and show the nest face on to the audience. The right hand assists in removing each cup placing it face (mouth) down onto the tabletop. In doing so, the

"Gallop move" (known to magicians) is executed. In fact, as a cup, containing a secreted ball, is inverted upon the table the contents remain within until the mouth of the cup hits the wooden surface. So, when the first cup, containing the hidden ball, is removed from the bottom it is inverted so that the ball drops with it, where it will end underneath.

The two remaining cups are removed singly in similar fashion these being placed in a line, mouths downward, alongisde the first one.

A ball, the first of three, is removed from the left pocket and held in the right hand. The right hand places it into the left when in reality it is retained in the right. The right hand, still concealing the hidden ball, lifts the cup on the left, tilting it forward toward the audience so to allow the ball to be released and enter beneath. In fact a pretense is made of the supposed ball in the left hand being placed under this cup when, in reality, it is contained within the right hand.

"Ladies and gentlemen . . . a transformation. Watch the ball travel from this cup to the one on the opposite side," says the performer as he points to the cups. Upon lifting the cup on the left the audience clearly see that it is empty. The center cup is also lifted and shown to be empty at this stage. In continuing the routine, the performer lifts the cup on the right using his right hand showing the ball has returned. While the audience's attention is directed toward this reproduction, the ball concealed in the right hand is allowed to drop inside the cup that is being gripped by the same hand (see Fig. 1).

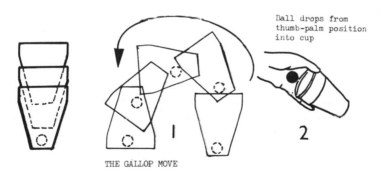

Ball drops from thumb-palm position into cup

THE GALLOP MOVE

**Figure 1.**

The gallop move is again executed as the cup is inverted upon the table, the ball secretly remaining beneath for a further effect.

The ball in view is taken in the right hand and then placed in the left [the "place-in move" (see Plate 15, page 101)].

"Which cup do you wish the ball to reappear under, Madam?" asks the performer, as he peers at his clenched fist.

45

The selected spectator has a choice of three cups. Should she point to either the left or center cup, the right hand, concealing the ball, goes toward the one of her choice, tilts the top toward the face of the audience releasing it beneath, thus making it suddenly reappear at this position. Should the spectator select the cup on the right, the left hand, which is empty at this stage, lifts it to reveal the one already there.

In either case, a ball must be loaded or hidden beneath the right cup, and should the latter position be chosen, the right hand, palming the ball, should load it inside at the same time the cup is lifted to make the reproduction. This loading procedure is standard practice among magicians. When the cup is lifted to reveal the ball, it is tilted downward so that the palmed ball in the right hand falls inside. The gallop move is executed, the mouth of the cup hitting the surface of the tabletop, concealing the ball inside.

With the hidden ball underneath the right cup, you are ready to present a penetration.

Place the visible ball on top of this cup. The remaining two cups are placed over this and "crashed" down to assist in a dramatic penetration, for, when the entire stack of cups is lifted, the ball is seen to be beneath, having apparently penetrated through.

Using the gallop move, once again the cups are displayed upon the table, with the secreted ball concealed under the center cup. The visible ball is vanished within the hands, in any of the methods previously described, but ultimately retained in the palm of the right hand. The center cup is lifted by the right hand, showing that the ball has made its appearance beneath. While the audience is appreciating this fact, the palmed ball is allowed to drop inside this cup, which is in "loading position," mouth upward, cup gripped firmly, ready to receive the ball. The cup, with the aid of the gallop move, is placed over the ball just produced. A second ball is removed from the left trouser pocket and vanished. The individual will have preferences in the methods used for such vanishes, but basically the right hand always secretly retains the ball.

The center cup is lifted to reveal the missing ball, now beside the first. With the cup gripped in the right hand, the palmed ball is loaded inside ready for the third and final production of the smaller balls. A third visible ball is removed from the pocket, vanished, and made to reappear under the center cup. The right hand, concealing the fourth ball, casually enters the right trouser pocket and discards it there, simultaneously obtaining one of the three larger balls in the finger-palm position. While this is being done, the left hand arranges the three smaller balls so that they are neatly displayed, one on top of each of the cups.

In continuing the sequence the final climax requires the conjurer to execute the "tip-off" move.

### "Tip-off" — Loading Move

This is executed only three times to bring about the production of the three large balls, one beneath each cup.

After you secret the first of the three large balls in the right hand, the same hand grips the base of the cup on the right and tilts it over toward the audience so to allow the small ball, resting on top, to fall into the awaiting cupped left hand. The gesture simply creates the impression that here is a practical way of dropping the ball from the top of the cup into the hand, without touching it. However, while you are presenting this flourish, the large ball concealed in the right hand is allowed to drop inside the cup. This is the loading position as used previously. This cup is immediately tilted backward so that it remains upright once again.

The smaller ball is taken in the right hand and pocketed in the right trouser pocket. Undercover, the second larger ball is finger-palmed while the performer points to the center cup and, in particular, to the ball resting upon it. The larger ball is loaded inside the cup as was done previously, and the smaller ball is left behind in the pocket.

The third and final large-sized ball is palmed and loaded inside in similar fashion to the preceding two. All three of the smaller balls have been pocketed. In placing the last of the three in your pocket, the fingers secretly gather these up into one wad, secreting them under the top lining of the trouser pocket.

The audience is led to believe that all three balls will vanish and reappear under their cups.

The performer reaches inside his trouser pocket, withdrawing the lining, showing that it is completely empty. *All three balls have completely vanished.*

Upon lifting the cups one by one, the surprise production of three large balls materializes.

The set of goblets, balls, and the magic wand can, if wished, be thoroughly examined, although this is not essential.

Once the student has mastered the various stages of the "Cups and Balls" he has in his repertoire one of the greatest miracles offered to the magical fraternity.

# THE MAGICIAN'S THUMB TIP

Of all the aids created and available to magicians, the "thumb tip," in my opinion, is by far the best.

Such a versatile little gimmick, it is an item that should never be seen but is there to assist the performer in a great number of ways.

The thumb tip is a hollow mold of a thumb. Available from magical dealers and some novelty stores, these are manufactured in plastic, metal, and heavy and soft rubber, and, in few cases, they are styled in plastic surgery to fit the thumb of the wearer.

The reader should be able to buy one to suit his own requirements. These vary in size, shape, and color. Unfortunately, it is almost impossible to obtain one that absolutely matches one's skin. Thumb tips have also been produced in black.

The tip should fit snugly over the thumb, yet should be loose enough for small items such as a silk, cigarette end, or a few grains of salt to be contained within.

While being used, the tip should never be seen by the audience. The thumb, wearing the tip, must always be positioned behind the fingers (see Fig. 2).

The three effects to follow have been carefully selected from many that can be presented by using the thumb tip. These have proved successful in the acts of many famous magicians.

## Vanishing a Lighted Cigarette in a Handkerchief

A lighted cigarette, borrowed from a member of the audience, is dropped into a spectator's handkerchief. Alarmed at the amount of smoke coming from the handkerchief, the performer quickly stubs out the cigarette and unfolds the handkerchief to show that it is unharmed. The cigarette has vanished completely, leaving no trace of damage to the borrowed handkerchief.

### The Working

The thumb tip should be worn on the right thumb.

A handkerchief is borrowed from a spectator and draped over the left fist (see Fig. 2). An indentation is made with the right thumb. When finally withdrawn, the thumb leaves the tip behind.

Borrowing a lighted cigarette, the performer drops it into the handkerchief (inside the tip). The burning cigarette is left there for a few seconds so that smoke pours from it in a most dramatic fashion.

Appearing to be alarmed over the situation, the performer com-

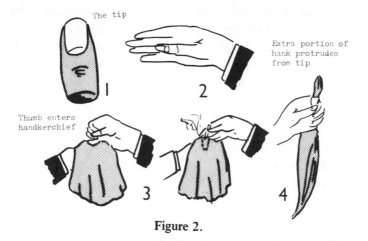

**Figure 2.**

mences to stub out the cigarette with his right thumb. In doing this, the cigarette is crushed and extinguished. In removing the thumb for the final time, the tip is stolen, the handkerchief opened and allowed to drape, showing no signs of damage. Meanwhile, the thumb wearing the tip is behind and out of view of the outstretched handkerchief. The cigarette has vanished, and the handkerchief, shown to be unharmed, is returned to its rightful owner.

The thumb tip is casually pocketed after the effect has been successfully presented.


### Burned and Restored Handkerchief

Using a similar plot, the center from a borrowed handkerchief is lighted and burned, and finally restored.

### The Working

The borrowed handkerchief is gripped from the center and allowed to hang. Its center is pulled through the clenched left fist (see Fig. 2). The handkerchief is removed from the fist and the procedure repeated, simply to establish the fact that a portion of the handkerchief must remain above the fist.

In executing the move a second time, the thumb tip, containing a small portion of material resembling that of the center from a handkerchief, is loaded inside the fist. It is this secret portion that is finally pulled up through the fist to appear as the center of the spectator's handkerchief.

Lighted by lighter or match, the portion in question is allowed to burn merrily until the flame dies. Restoring the handkerchief to its normal state, the thumb quickly enters the tip, taking this and the burned pieces of paper away. The handkerchief is displayed between the hands with thumb tip concealed behind same. The handkerchief is shown to be restored and quite unharmed.

## Pass the Salt

Here is another classic effect using the thumb tip.

From a shaker, salt is poured into the left fist. It vanishes and reappears in the right hand.

### The Working

The thumb tip is worn on the right thumb.

In presentation, the left hand is shown empty, being made into a fist. The right hand introduces the thumb tip into the left during the display. It is while the fingers of the right hand assist in cupping those of the left that the tip is stolen.

The right hand pours salt from a shaker inside the clenched fist (really inside the tip).

Pushing the salt inside with the right thumb, the tip is stolen away.

The left hand is opened slowly, the fingers being parted one by one.

The salt is seen to have vanished. Clenching a fist, the right hand fingers secretly pull off the tip so that it is now within the hand. While you invert the fist, the salt is made to pour from the hand, thus making its reappearance.

The thumb tip is secretly forced onto the thumb so that the hands can be quickly shown to be empty.

## SUPER SPONGES

Of all the close-up effects I have seen, I think this, the famous sponge ball trick, is my favorite. Ideally suited for both close-up and stage work, its presentation is quick, slick, and visual, involving participation with the audience.

### The Effect

Sponge balls vanish and reappear under the most impossible conditions. One even vanishes to reappear within the spectator's hand—a most surprising climax!

## The Apparatus Required

Although I have referred to sponge balls, these can be squares cut from synthetic nylon foam bath sponges. In fact, sponge balls are professionally manufactured and sold by United States and European magical dealers and are available in various sizes and colors.

Should the student wish to manufacture his own, these should be cut from sponge using a multipurpose knife. With a sharp blade, trim off the corners and continue snipping with a pair of scissors until the ball is formed. Keep the sponge on the move, snipping tiny segments away from the surface of the sponge. It is, however, essential that the balls are of identical size, for if these should vary, your audience will soon detect the difference between a ball that has been made to vanish and one that is made to reappear.

You require four such balls.

In setting up the routine, one of the balls is secretly finger-palmed as already described.

## The Routine

The right hand, concealing the fourth ball, points to the three visible balls that rest upon the table. The same hand lifts up the first visible ball and places it into the left hand. The second ball is lifted and placed beside it, but in doing so, the fourth unseen palmed ball is also released.

Because of the nature of the material used, sponge being springy and flexible, the second ball, alongside the newly introduced fourth ball, appears as one when both are pressed and forced into the hand. The move is a quick one, the ball(s) going into the left hand. The left hand is closed to form a fist. The open right hand lifts up the third remaining ball, placing it inside the trouser pocket.

"Flip," says the conjurer. Upon opening his left hand he allows the balls to roll onto the table, revealing that the third ball has apparently returned to the others.

Meanwhile, the right hand, which is casually resting inside the trouser pocket, retaining a ball in finger palm position, is removed while misdirection is made toward the left hand displaying the visible balls.

The entire procedure is repeated. A ball is pocketed, made to vanish and then to reappear with the other two already gripped within the hand.

## The Climax

With the fourth ball still retained in finger-palm position, and in the right hand, you are set to complete what will appear to be a most accomplished feat, for the vanished ball will ultimately reappear within a spectator's hand.

The setup is as before. Three sponge balls are lined up on the table surface.

The right hand, concealing the fourth ball, lifts up the first visible ball from the table and asks a spectator to hold it firmly in his hand. It is dropped inside. The right hand now lifts up the second visible ball, and with his left hand firmly supporting the spectator's wrist, adds the additional ball so that is is forced into the awaiting hand.

As both balls, placed as one, hit the spectator's palm, the performer assists in closing the fist. At this stage the spectator will not realize that he is, in fact, holding three balls and not two as he is supposed to be.

On this occasion the vanish of the ball varies. Since the ball will not be required for further use, it is definitely placed inside the trouser pocket where it remains. However, the old "pocket dodge move," known to magicians for many years, comes into action. In placing the ball inside the pocket, the hand brings it up to the top of the lining where it is lodged. The hand is removed and shown to be empty.

"Flip," says the performer, as he places his hand inside the pocket, grips the base of the lining, and pulls it out. With the inside lining hanging from the trousers, the ball is hidden and trapped beneath and toward the top of the inside pocket. A neat yet simple vanish.

The performer requests that the spectator open his hand, and the missing ball reappears, having made its way to join the others held within the clenched fist.

While sponge balls or squares have proved to be most practical for the presentation of this routine, sugar lumps are just as effective, if not easier to obtain. However, because of the size of the balls used, the audience will credit the performer with additional skill, and it will be possible to present the routine before larger crowds.


## THE CLASSIC EGG BAG

Arnold de Biere featured the classic egg bag in the famous music halls, while The Great Levante toured the world featuring, among his many illusions, the trick with the little cloth bag and an egg.

During presentation, an egg appears inside an empty cloth bag, vanishes, and reappears. At one particular stage, the audience believes that they see the performer "steal" the egg from the bag, placing it beneath his armpit, but they are proved wrong, for it is nowhere to be seen. The cloth bag is turned inside out and twisted between the hands, proving it is again completely empty. Yet, within seconds, a spectator from the audience can place his hand inside to reproduce the egg from the bag.

### The Apparatus Required

You will need specially made cloth bag (see Fig. 3).

The bag is faked, having a secret pocket sewn within, across the full length of the side of the bag. The pocket has an opening toward the bottom. This is where the egg is concealed.

You will also require an imitation egg. Such are sold commercially by magical dealers and joke novelty suppliers. A plastic or heavy rubber egg is most practical, although one made in china, as used by farmers tempting their hens to lay, is acceptable. It is not advisable to use a blown egg for obvious reasons.

The pocket

Side view
Egg drops from
pocket to base
of bag

**Figure 3.**

### The Setup

Prior to the performance have the egg concealed within the pocket in the bag.

### The Working

Lift the bag from the table. The fingers of the right hand grip the egg through the cloth of the bag, retaining it there so that the bag itself can be turned inside out. The pocket is always kept toward the rear and away from the audience. The bag is refolded to its original position.

In showing both inside and out to be empty the performer is able to commence the routine that follows.

"Ladies and gentlemen, a simple cloth bag. [show the bag, inside and out].

"But, by uttering three simple words . . . CLUCK . . . CLUCK . . . CLUCK . . . something will surely appear inside."

As the performer recites these lines his empty right hand reaches inside to produce the egg, which has been allowed to drop from the secret pocket, because of releasing pressure.

"An egg . . . well, I for one know that this is a most egg-straordinary trick, one that I could not egg-xaggerate in any way. I do not wish to egg-spose the secret of this trick to anyone, for I hope this entire egg-stravaganza will be as egg-citing as it possibly can. Enough about such 'eggy' words. . . . Let's take the egg and place it inside the bag [this is done]. Turn the bag inside out to show that the egg has vanished.

"A snap of the fingers [snap] and we reverse the bag [done]. No egg . . . egg-straordinary indeed, you may say. Let's have a look inside. It's a clever trick, but please don't let me become egg-otistical over such matters."

At this point the bag has been turned inside out, proving its emptiness, the egg being concealed within the pocket. The bag is held high, the egg naturally dropping from the inside pocket so that it lies at the bottom.

"Sir, would you kindly assist me [pointing to a spectator] . . . say my magic words if you can . . . you know the ones . . . CLUCK . . . CLUCK . . . CLUCK, or something like that!" The spectator, assisting in providing the particular sounds, is asked to place his hand inside the bag and remove the egg.

Asked to replace the egg inside the bag the spectator makes sure it is dropped inside. The performer's hand is seen to enter the bag for a second or two, coming out clenched with what appears to be the egg inside. The move is supposed to be a secret one but is exaggerated by the performer for best effect. In fact the hand is empty but is placed beneath the armpit where the egg appears to be now hidden. The performer announces that he will make the egg disappear from inside the bag. The bag is turned inside out, twisted, and finally unwinded, the concealed egg falling from the pocket.

"An empty bag, ladies and gentlemen, and just like a balloon, without a skin . . . nothing at all!"

What? It's under my arm sir? . . . don't be silly, of course it's not . . . I never carry eggs under my arm. You are convinced it is under my arm sir? . . . very well, I will prove you wrong for the final and last time . . . and that's final, if you see what I mean," says the performer.

During this comedy dialogue the performer proves that the egg is not under the arm by lifting his right hand high into the air. The audience is not impressed by his actions, knowing fully that it is actually contained under his left arm. However, the performer proves this wrong also, for he lifts both arms high to prove that the egg is nowhere to be seen.

Showing that the bag is still quite empty by turning it inside out and back again, he asks the spectator to make a very big CLUCK on this special occasion. Indeed it works wonders, for when the spectator sounds his voice and then reaches inside the bag, he finds the missing egg.

This is a basic routine for the egg bag. Some performers go as far as stamping hard upon the bag, avoiding the obvious portion that contains the egg, to prove its emptiness, but this is not necessary.

The egg bag is a classic, one trick that still remains with us after so many years. Do it justice by presenting it properly in the manner in which it should be presented.

## PRODUCING A RABBIT FROM A HAT

The magician has always been associated with the famous production, that of a live rabbit from an empty hat. Although being performed on countless occasions, the fact is that the majority of magicians do not normally include this particular trick in their acts. To most, may I coin a phrase, it is old hat!

Relying upon an old principle, this version still remains superior to others.

The performer displays his empty hat from which a live rabbit is magically produced.

### The Apparatus Required

A top hat (solid or opera).

A simple bag, made from a piece of cloth measuring twenty inches square (see Fig. 4).

Onto the four corners are sewn curtain rings.

A nail or screw, secured to the back of a draped table, is also essential to the working of this trick. A temporary suction hook, obtainable from most do-it-yourself shops, is just as practical, if not

Bag, containing rabbit at
rear of table, on nail-head
or hook

Lifting the hat, the
load-bag swings inwards,
inside the hat

1

2

**Figure 4.**

more sensible, should the performer wish to remove it easily without damaging the surface of the table material.

### The Setup

The rabbit is comfortably placed inside the cloth square, the corners of which are brought together. The curtain rings are engaged over the hook or nail-head behind the draped table. In this position, the rabbit will stay undisturbed, until required. The hat, with its mouth downward, should be on the table.

### Working and Presentation

In presentation, the performer picks up the hat and displays its inside to be empty, replacing it mouth downward onto the table.

In lifting the hat once more from the table, the fingers of the left hand grasp hold of the brim, while the thumb disengages the rings from the hook toward the back. The action that follows should appear solely of the hat being turned mouth upward. The left hand pivots the hat over (see Fig. 4) at the same time allowing the "load bag" to comfortably come with it. When upright, the hat now secretly contains the bag and rabbit.

The corners of the cloth square automatically drop open allowing the rabbit to be produced from the hat. The cloth holder is left behind.

You have just produced a live rabbit from a hat!

## THE FAMOUS MULTIPLYING BILLIARD BALLS

From midair a billiard ball is produced. It multiplies until the

56

performer grips four balls between his fingers. The balls vanish singly, transpose, and reappear in a most uncanny fashion.

### The Apparatus Required

The set is comprised of three solid balls and one shell (shallowed-out half ball). The shell is made to fit over any of the three balls. I suggest that the balls should be painted in red laquer, the color proving to be the most practical, enabling audiences large and small to see these clearly during performance. A silk handkerchief is also required.

### The Setup

Place a ball, with the shell over it, in your right trouser pocket. Inside your left jacket pocket place another ball. The third ball is placed inside your left trouser pocket together with the silk handkerchief.

### Working and Presentation

The right hand, casually resting in the right trouser pocket, is removed, palming the ball, with shell over same.

This ball (with shell) is plucked out of the air and shown on both sides as one ball.

Held between the thumb and index finger of the right hand the middle finger is lowered so as to pivot the solid ball out from the shell. From the front view the performer appears to be holding two solid balls, these being displayed between the fingers.

The left hand comes up to supposedly take away the ball that is

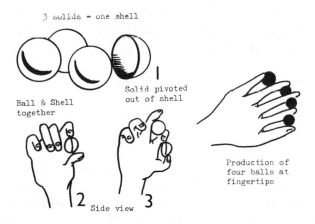

3 solids - one shell

Ball & Shell together

Solid pivoted out of shell

2    Side view    3

Production of four balls at fingertips

**Figure 5.**

gripped between the first and second fingers, but in fact, simply forms a shield to cover what then follows as an unseen move. The hand makes a clutching motion, allowing the ball to pivot back inside the shell. The clutched fist, supposedly containing the ball, is brought away from the right hand, where one solid ball appears to remain, this being gripped between the thumb and first finger.

### The Vanish

The left hand is slowly opened to reveal its emptiness, the ball having mysteriously vanished. At the same time, the empty hand reaches inside the left trouser pocket, removing the already planted ball, using it as a reproduction effect. As this ball is being positioned between the first and second fingers, the ball within the shell is quickly pivoted out, thus filling this available space. Three balls have been magically produced at this particular stage of the routine.

The left hand shields the center ball, pretending to remove it form its position but, in making a false motion of grasping it, allows the ball to pivot back inside the shell.

### Another Vanish

This time the performer pretends to place the ball inside his mouth, and, as the clenched fist makes this motion, the tongue presses against the side of the cheek giving the impression of a ball being contained in the mouth. The hand is shown to be empty. The first finger of the left hand pushes the "bulge" inward, making it appear that the performer has swallowed the ball. The left hand reaches inside the left hand jacket pocket, reproducing the ball already there. Placing it firmly between the third and little fingers, the three balls are shown on both sides. The final fourth ball is produced from within the shell, as before, using the pivoting action, so that it now takes place between the first and second fingers.

The balls are vanished one by one in the following manner.

The right hand is shown to contain and display the four balls. Shaken in the air, the hand appears to be holding one less, the ball between the first and second fingers being allowed to pivot inside the shell, thus leaving three in view. Both sides of the balls are repeatedly shown. In checking that the balls are correctly positioned and rearranging these so that they appear as in Figure 5, the fingers of the left hand "steal" the ball from within the shell. In fact, this ball is allowed to drop out of the shell and into the awaiting clenched fist. While the right hand makes a second vanish, the left secretly pockets the unwanted ball.

The left hand removes the ball from the second and third fingers so that it is now above the ball with the shell over same.

In doing this, the left hand "steals" away the ball from within the shell (similar procedure as before).

The left hand, formed as a fist, is dropped to the side of the trousers, with the back of the hand toward the audience.

Similarly, the right hand, containing what appears to be two solid balls, of which one is really the shell, is lowered to the right hand side of the trousers.

With a throwing motion of the right hand, the solid ball is shown to have vanished, it being pivoted inside the shell. Simultaneously, the palmed ball within the left hand is produced, proving a rather neat and visual transposition.

Place this ball above the shell, and undercover, steal away the one that is inside the shell. Reach inside the jacket pocket to remove the silk handkerchief, leaving the ball there. The left hand holds the silk by one corner, draping it over both balls, and then reaches beneath, supposedly to take one away. In fact the ball is pivoted into the shell, the left hand coming away empty but making a pretense of holding it firmly.

The fingers of the left hand are slowly opened to show that the ball has vanished.

The handkerchief is removed, showing that only one ball remains, and it can (along with the shell that covers it) be vanished in any of the methods already described in the sleight-of-hand section of this book.

The handkerchief should be pocketed prior to the vanish being made, and the routine should end, as at the beginning, with the performer's hands being completely empty!

The pivoting move may at first seem awkward in the hands of the beginner, but I can assure readers that with constant practice, preferably in front of a mirror, it is possible for anyone to master the moves and present a polished performance.

## THE CHINESE LINKING RINGS

Definitely one of the greatest mysteries ever created, the "Chinese Linking Rings" has been performed by magicians from all over the world.

The illusion is incredible. Single rings link, unlink, join together in symphony, and finally come falling apart.

## The Apparatus Required

Although a professional set of linking rings can be bought from a magical dealer, it is possible for the individual to manufacture his own. If he is proficient in working with metal, he will be able to make the necessary apparatus.

### The Set of Rings

The set consists of eight rings
These are comprised of the following:

> Two single rings
> A set of two rings permanently linked together
> A set of three rings permanently linked together
> The "key" ring ( a ring with a gap)

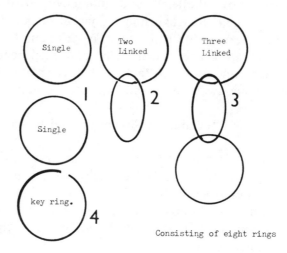

Consisting of eight rings

**Figure 6.**

### The Setup

Have the rings resting upon a table or over the rung of a chair. They should be set in this order, from the bottom of the stack: the key, one single, the chain of three, the chain of two, and one single. It is important that the performer pick up the set in this order.

### Working and Presentation

"A trick from China, as old as magic itself, it is called the Chinese

Rings. Before your very eyes you will see these solid rings do incredible things. Ladies and gentlemen, eight solid steel rings. Let me count them."

In counting the rings, the "drop count" is used.

The move is executed by bringing the right hand up toward the rings, catching the first single ring, which is allowed to drop from the others. The right hand is lowered slightly so that the audience can clearly see that it is separate from the others of the set.

Next, the two linked rings are allowed to drop singly into the awaiting right hand, which, as before, lowers.

Similarly, the following three rings (linked) are dropped so that they appear to fall one at a time into the right hand, alongside the others. Finally, the key ring is lowered and counted as eight—eight solid and separate rings.

In transferring the rings back to the left hand, these remain in their original order. The gap in the key ring is always to the top and covered by the thumb of the left hand during the presentation.

### Linking Two Rings

The first single ring is removed from the front by the right hand and is "crashed" against the others. Simultaneously, the first finger of the left hand allows the first of the two linked rings to fall. The illusion is somewhat created of the single ring being crashed against the others, then falling so that it hangs from the set. This ring, now linked to the other, is removed, displaying a perfectly coupled pair. These are handed to a spectator for thorough examination.

### Linking Three More Rings

The loose single ring, still in front position, is removed by the right hand and, again, crashed against the front of the set. The first ring of the set of three linked ones is allowed to drop and hang. Again the same loose ring is removed and crashed against the others, and the second ring of this three falls to make its appearance.

The hanging rings are taken away from the set and shown as three linked together, these being handed to another spectator for examination.

The performer, at this stage, is left holding two single rings, one of which is the key.

Holding these in both hands, the performer rubs them together, engaging the solid ring onto and over the key ring. The rubbing motion should continue for a short period even after the rings are actually linked together. Suddenly, the solid ring is allowed to drop so that it becomes linked to the other (key).

Referring to the first spectator holding the chain of two, the performer requests him to repeat his actions. The two linked rings held by the performer are positioned in front of the body. "Please rub your rings together, sir, just as I am doing now," he says, as he carries out the action.

While the spectator duplicates the performer's moves, the performer's rings become parted. The rings held by the spectator still remain linked and cannot be budged apart. This is an amusing scene and one that has to be witnessed to be believed.

The single ring, resting over the performer's arm during this sequence, is removed, and now all three rings are linked together, both solids entering the key to make it possible.

Asking the second spectator to repeat his actions, the performer gathers his set of three rings together. The spectator does likewise.

First, one loose ring is removed from the three held by the performer. Alas, the spectator finds it impossible to do the same, but normally tries hard to achieve this problem.

A second ring (key), is removed, thumb covering the gap, and the third ring is thrown into the air to prove that all three are completely separate at this stage.

The spectator's rings still remain linked.

Requesting the first spectator to hand over his set of linked rings, these are taken by the performer, who rubs them against the already linked ones in his hands. Under cover of the rubbing motion, all three become linked to the others, being forced over the gap in the key.

The key ring is gripped so that the others hang from it.

In continuing the routine, the chain of three linked rings is taken from the second spectator and, likewise, is placed alongside the others, one being forced over the key, as before.

At this stage the performer displays the entire set of rings, seven hanging from the uppermost ring (the key) gripped in the hand.

"Ladies and gentlemen, eight solid rings of steel. In my hands they have become soft as jelly. But, let me prove once again that we have, just as we started with, eight solid, separate rings".

Holding the set high above his head and away from his body, the performer prepares for the climax of the trick. The rings suddenly fall singly from the hands onto the floor.

Undercover, the gap in the key ring is opened so that the others automatically scatter to the floor. The key ring is likewise dropped with the others.

Although this classic effect and routine is easy to perform, a certain amount of practice, skill, and dexterity are required so that the performer becomes proficient in the handling of the rings.

## THE FOUR ACE TRICK

Many different versions of the famous "Four Ace Trick" have been devised and performed successfully by card experts the world over. It is a fascinating card sequence, one using a borrowed deck if wished. In this particular version, simplicity is the keynote, for we have eliminated the difficult sleight-of-hand moves that are so normally used in achieving the effect. Within a quarter of an hour the student will have learned one of the greatest classics of card magic—a simple trick using the four aces.

*The Effect*

From a borrowed deck of cards, the performer removes the four aces.

"Watch the aces closely," he says, as he carefully places them on top of the pack. With faces down, the four aces are dealt from the top of the deck, onto the table so that they form a line.

The fourth ace is reversed, just to prove, like the others, that it is really an ace and nothing less.

Next, three indifferent cards are dealt and placed on top of the first ace. The same procedure is adopted with the remaining three, these being covered by three indifferent cards.

"Birds of a feather . . . flock together," quips the performer, as he reverses the first stock of four cards, showing that the ace is no longer there, having completely vanished!

The cards of the second and third piles are similarly reversed only to show that their aces are missing as well. In reversing the fourth pile of cards, all four aces are seen to have magically gathered together.

The deck of cards is immediately handed out for examination, and because it is a borrowed one, no one could possibly suspect any unforeseen trickery on the part of the performer.

*Working and Presentation*

Should you be in someone's home and are asked to perform a trick, borrow a deck of cards. Riffle through these and locate the four aces, removing these from the deck. The aces are placed on the front of the deck, which is fanned toward the audience. While displaying the cards,

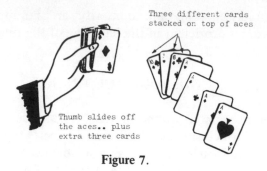

Three different cards
stacked on top of aces

Thumb slides off
the aces.. plus
extra three cards

**Figure 7.**

the left hand closes up the deck, the thumb pushing forward the next three cards. In removing the four aces from the front of the deck the additional three cards are secretly hidden behind the stack. This means that when the aces are placed on *top* of the deck, these indifferent cards are above and now the top cards.

"This experiment uses the four aces of the deck . . . clubs, hearts, spades and diamonds. I deal them like so [in a line]."

The cards are dealt from the top of the pack, face down, from left to right, so that the four remain in a line. The first three cards, supposedly aces to the audience, are, in fact, indifferent cards. The fourth card in the line is a genuine ace, the first, in fact, of the four, the remaining three now being on top of the deck. The fourth card is reversed at this stage, proving it is an ace.

On top of this displayed ace are dealt the next three cards, all face down (all aces).

"It's really amazing, ladies and gentlemen, just how cards do travel. Let me prove a point!"

A similar procedure to that of dealing three indifferent cards onto a pile is executed so that all three supposed aces are covered.

"I snap the first pile of cards with my fingers and find . . . [reversed] the ace has vanished. The same applies to the second, and third piles, the ace vanishing into thin air . . . remarkable. I wonder where the aces could have possibly traveled to?"

Pointing to the fourth pile of cards, the performer smiles, reversing these to reveal the four aces, clubs, hearts, spades, and diamonds. Like birds of a feather, they have indeed come together!

The deck of cards can be handed out for examination should the performer feel this is necessary. By all means, he can leave it on the table for those mistrusting persons who are always out to catch the performer and steal some of his success.

# 4  Close-up Magic

By far, the most popular branch of our craft is close-up magic, or micro-magic as it is known in parts of Europe, because of its simplicity: mysteries performed at close quarters.

In this section, tricks and routines using common everyday objects such as match boxes, cigarettes, dice, cards, pencils, pins, and finger rings are used to good advantage, involving little or no expense.

Easily prepared and put to practice, these minor miracles can be performed almost anywhere: in the bar, hotel, club, or office, or simply at home.

The student wishing to learn more about the preparation and requirements of such a show should refer to page 40, which covers many aspects of this type of entertainment.

Sleight-of-hand is sometimes involved in close-up work, but as a branch of its own, it has its individual chapter.

For the impromptu bar trick or the close-up teaser to fool one's friends, this chapter contains some new and original items, never before published.

## NEAT COIN CHANGE

A borrowed coin, resting on top of a matchbox, when tipped into the hand, mysteriously changes to one of a different value and design. The change is sudden, and the method is simplicity itself.

### The Apparatus Required

A match box. As illustrated, a slit, large enough to allow a coin to slide through, is cut along one edge of the inner tray.

A small piece of candle wax or soap.

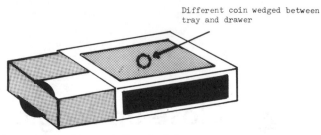

Different coin wedged between tray and drawer

Original coin slides out through slot

**Figure 8.**

### The Setup

Refill the matchbox with matches. Secretly conceal a coin, different from the one you intend borrowing later, inside the matchbox, which should be positioned on the table.

A small portion of wax or soap should be smeared on top of the match box, in the central area.

### Working and Presentation

The performer borrows a coin from a member of his audience, making sure that it differs in value to the one already secreted inside the box. The coin is placed on top of the box and onto the portion of wax or soap where it adheres.

The match box is held between the thumb and forefinger of the right hand. In tipping the top of the box toward the left hand as though to allow the coin to drop, in fact it remains secure by the aid of the wax. The action of tipping the box in this manner allows the planted one to slide through the slit in the tray, into the awaiting hand. The entire movement looks natural enough to be convincing. The match box is acually pocketed.

Upon opening his hand, the coin is seen to have changed its value.

Should the performer wish to be extra clever, an additional unfaked match box can be in the jacket pocket, so that when the faked model is pocketed, this one can be exchanged and later, brought into view for examination.

No doubt, the spectator will not complain in accepting the changed coin, providing it is one higher in value.

## REVOLVING JOKER

"Watch the joker," says the performer, as he displays it with a metal paper clip fastened to its side.

"In placing it into the center of the deck, face upward alongside the others, I shall try to make it reverse itself."

The deck of cards is squared up and turned over. True enough, when fanned, only one card is reversed, the joker, still displaying its paper clip. The deck can be thoroughly examined.

### The Apparatus Required

A regular deck of cards. A paper clip.

### The Setup

Prior to performance, remove both jokers from the deck, and placing them back to back, secure them squarely with the paper clip, which should protrude from the top edges of the cards. Place the joker(s) in the center of the deck.

### Working and Presentation

Fan the deck, showing the position of the joker, and emphasize the fact that, for ease in finding it again, you have fastened a paper clip to its top. Square up the deck, reverse this, and fan the cards with backs showing.

The only card that appears to be reversed is the joker, thanks to the setup, using two, backed together. The clip is removed, the top card of the two is taken from the deck, which can then be handed to members of the audience for examination.

Here is a self-working trick that can be presented ad lib while using a borrowed deck of cards. Providing you have a few seconds beforehand to make the necessary preparation, it can be a winner. It is certainly one of my favorites!

## IMPROMPTU RISING PEN

A borrowed ball-point pen, held in the hand, rises at command in a most spooky fashion. The effect can be repeated several times, the pen then being returned to its owner.

### The Apparatus Required

A thin elastic band.

### The Setup

The elastic band is secretly placed over the forefinger of the right hand, hanging from there toward the palm, which is held away from the audience during the routine.

### Working and Presentation

The performer requests several members of his audience to remove their ball-point pens. Studying these, he selects just one, putting an influence upon it.

"This gentleman's pen reacts to my commands," he says.

In fact, while selecting one of the pens, the performer makes sure that he accepts one that has the standard hooked top. Most pens are made in this manner.

In placing the pen into the right hand, the hanging elastic band is engaged into the hook as illustrated. The elastic band is brought around the base, up against the shaft of the pen, until it nearly reaches the point. Held firmly in this position, and with release of tension, the pen commences to rise slowly and quickly as the performer so wishes. The pen spookily rises through the clenched fist and, when pushed back, repeats its actions.

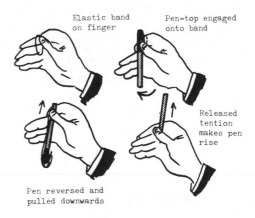

Elastic band
on finger

Pen-top engaged
onto band

Released
tention
makes pen
rise

Pen reversed and
pulled downwards

**Figure 9.**

The entire effect is self-working, and after repetition of effect, the elastic band can be easily disconnected from the hook of the pen, which is then returned to its owner.


## ON STRIKE

Here is a cute, impromptu sequence using matches, which appear to behave in an uncanny fashion.

A match is removed from a match box, is lighted, and then is extinguished. It is suddenly restruck to produce a flame.

A second match is seen not to be alive, yet immediately takes to fire. This same spent match is struck again to light once more! Can this be "light entertainment"?

### *The Apparatus Required*

The matches used are specially faked to produce the most uncanny results, as mentioned above. All are converted from genuine live matches.

Match number one: the restriking match.

This match is made from two live match sticks. As illustrated, both are cut in half, spliced, and glued together with a strong glue, resulting in a double-sided match stick, with two live ends. Alternatively, a straight cut, with both pieces of the matchsticks being fastened together with clear tape, would be second best, adequate enough to function during the routine.

Match number two: the nonstrike match—that lights!

Prepare this special match as above, using two, these being joined together as before. Dampen one head so that it cannot be struck.

Match number three: Dead, come-alive match.

To prepare this match, strike one, let it burn for a few seconds, then

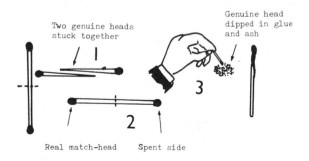

**Figure 10.**

69

extinguish the flame. Apply a fish glue substance onto its head and lower parts. Roll these parts into an ashtray that contains ash, so that particles cling to the applied surfaces. In effect, it will appear as a dead, spent match.

### Working and Presentation

Match number three, the dead one, is planted in an nearby ashtray, prior to the performance taking place. The remaining two match sticks are placed inside a match box alongside the others.

In presenting the experiments, the performer first removes a match from the box, looks at it, strikes it against the box surface, and blows out the flame. While holding the match stick between the finger and thumb of the right hand, pivot it around so that the duplicate head comes into view. The match stick can be immediately restruck to prove that it can be lighted once again.

The performer, appearing to be puzzled over this occurrence, removes yet another match from the box (match number two nonstrike match).

Striking it against the side of the box many times, it refuses to be lighted, thanks to the dampened head. A similar pivot move is executed to bring the live head to the upper position, from where it can be struck to produce a flame. This spent match is dropped into the ashtray.

Puzzled over the various antics that the match sticks have encountered, the performer gropes for the spent match inside the ashtray. In reality, he removes the specially prepared and planted one, which provides the climax to this little sequence. In picking up the ash-covered match stick, he strikes its head against the surface of the matchbox. It lights!

"What a performance . . . ladies and gentlemen . . . and all just to light my cigarette." The performer lights his cigarette from this match and finally retires.

Certainly, a most unusual little sequence, but one that can be presented anywhere, at anytime, and without too much preparation.

### CORKED TIP—FIRST!

A cork-tipped cigarette, pushed through the fist, reverses itself again and again. Finally the cigarette is handed out for examination.

Sliding sand-paper tip.

**Figure 11.**

### The Apparatus Required

Two cigarettes, one tipped, one untipped.

A small piece of fine sandpaper. White adhesive tape and some glue.

You require an oblong piece of fine sandpaper, ¾" x 1½" long. Roll it into a tube, around the circumference of the cigarette itself, so that a resemblance of a cork tip results. The paper is glued in position, and this tubelike tip can slide to and fro along the length of the untipped cigarette. So that it is not possible for it to slide completely off the ends of the cigarette, a piece of white adhesive tape is finally wound around both ends as illustrated. The sliding tip, in fact, is trapped between both taped ends.

You now have a perfectly ordinary looking cigarette that has a removable tip. This tip can be transferred from one end to the other while the cigarette is being pushed through the clenched fist.

### The Setup

The unfaked tipped cigarette is inside the right jacket pocket. The faked one, with the sliding tip, is placed among other genuine cigarettes within a cigarette pack.

### Working and Presentation

The faked cigarette is removed from the pack. Showing his left hand to be empty, the performer forms a fist. Displaying the cigarette so that it is obvious to the audience that the tipped end enters the fist, the performer commences to push the cigarette in. The thumb and first finger of the right hand retain a grip on the tip so that when it is finally pushed through the fist the tip will be on the opposite end.

The cigarette is removed to show that it has actually reversed itself, the tip now being at the opposite end.

Repeated, the effect requires a similar technique.

It is, however, advisable to the performer not to present the effect

71

more than three times, otherwise the method may become obvious if repeated further.

While the cigarette is being pushed into the left fist for the third and final time, the right hand casually goes to the right jacket pocket, retains the unfaked tipped cigarette within the thumb and finger palm (see Plate 35) and brings it out. When the faked cigarette has been reversed for the last time and displayed in the left hand, the right, palming the unfaked one, comes in front, pivots down the faked one while bringing into view the genuine. To the audience, the right hand supposedly comes forward and removes the cigarette from the left. The genuine cigarette is now thrown down upon the table as being the one used throughout the effect.

## DICE—BLACK AND WHITE

Three dice, two black with white spots, one white with black spots, and three dice shakers are used to create a most unusual effect.

This assumes a sort of "Find the Lady" routine, the performer requesting a spectator to assist him in the presentation of the trick.

All three dice are covered by their shakers and rearranged so that it is impossible for the performer is able to reveal the location of the odd die, the one that is white bearing black spots. The experiment can be repeated several times without the audience being aware of the secret involved.

### The Apparatus Required

Three dice: two black with white spots, one white with black spots.
Three dice shakers.
A length of fine hair or thread.

### The Setup

Attach the length of hair of thread, by aid of clear adhesive tape, to the base of the odd die. Use a dark surface to work upon, such as a mat, cloth, or cover.

### Working and Presentation

The three dice are set in front of their shakers.
Pointing out that one of the dice is different, being odd, in fact, the performer requests a spectator to cover each with a shaker and then

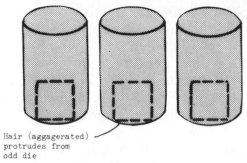

Hair (aggagerated)
protrudes from
odd die

**Figure 12.**

rearrange the positions until it is impossible for anyone to locate any one die. The performer can leave the room at this point or be heavily blindfolded so that there is no possibility of him watching the shakers being rearranged.

After the spectator has arranged the shakers in a row, the performer has only to casually peer at the shaker that has the piece of fine hair protruding from underneath. Such a clue becomes obvious after a certain amount of practice, for the performer knows what to look for and find it easily.

This pleasing and entertaining effect can be repeated several times, but like all magical presentations, the surprise element may somewhat disappear should the principle be carelessly used.

## UPSIDE DOWN

Here is a teaser with a piece of paper. Introduced anytime, at a party, in the bar, or while entertaining a few friends at home, it offers an interesting problem, which the performer can solve and demonstrate immediately.

A spectator is asked to write, in capital letters, the words: UPSIDE DOWN on the center of the paper.

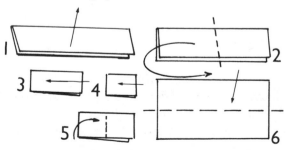

**Figure 13.**

73

The paper is folded so the words are out of view, yet, when reopened, apparently in a similar manner, they appear to be upside down. The words have actually reversed.

To accomplish this small yet effective feat the performer requires a piece of paper approximately the same size as a dollar bill.

The secret lies within the method of folding, and so, with the piece of paper bearing the words in the upright position, commence by:

1. Showing the piece of paper.
2. Fold it in half, lengthwise, then from right to left as indicated.
3. The result. Continue to fold from right to left.
4. The result. Reopen the folded packet. Arrow pointing right shows how the folds should be made. A repeat procedure is executed, the folds being opened to the right.
5. The result. One final opening to the right, then the top portion folded downward.
6. The words UPSIDE DOWN are seen to be just this, reversed in the true sense of the words.

This is not designed to be a world-beating mystery, but a cute, impromptu stunt that is capable of livening up any party at a moment's notice.


## FLOWER SHOW

Here is a cute pocket effect using a gardening theme.

From a packet of illustrated cards, each bearing the design of an empty vase, several are removed, spectators placing their signatures upon them.

While the spectators hold their cards, the performer spinkles "imaginary" garden dust over these.

Upon reversing their cards, the spectators find that their empty vases now contain flowers, neatly illustrated on top, with signatures still intact.


### The Apparatus Required

A number of white cards measuring 5" x 3".

On the surfaces of a few, draw similar shaped vases, so that these occupy the bottom half of the cards only. Different flowers are illustrated on the upper portions of the cards, these appearing to emerge from the vases.

You will also require a blank half-card.

Half blank card

**Figure 14.**

### The Setup

The illustrated cards are placed on top of the packet of otherwise blank cards. A wide elastic band, placed around central position, not only secures the cards, but assists in the working of the trick. The blank half-card is secured under the elastic band so that it covers the illustrated flower portion. The first picture on top of the packet then appears to be that of an empty vase.

### Working and Presentation

The stack of cards is removed from the pocket and displayed, emphasis being made upon the uppermost card, that bearing the illustration of an empty vase.

In introducing the gardening theme, the performer states that he intends holding a flower show, and in doing so, asks four spectators to assist.

One by one the spectators are asked to accept a card.

In supplying these, each spectator is requested to sign his name somewhere on the bottom portion. It is this portion that is held by the performer in the removing of the entire card, for when it has been pulled away from the others, the complete picture showing the flowers in the vase is on one side. Placed face down upon the table, each card is sprinkled with imaginary garden dust and the performer goes through various antics as though it were being applied.

When the spectators reverse their cards, all are seen to have flowers emerging from their vases. Magic gardening indeed!

## MYSTIC RING

This unusual mystery is sure to entertain any type of audience.

A borrowed finger ring is placed underneath a pocket handkerchief, which is then held by a spectator. A small brass bell, with missing clapper, is placed upon the performer's palm.

Suddenly, the handkerchief is snatched away, the ring mysteriously vanishing and then reappearing beneath the bell. A different "ring" is sounded, for while the bell rings again, it now contains the spectator's finger ring underneath.

### The Apparatus Required

A pocket handkerchief.
A curtain ring, measuring approximately ¾" in diameter.
A brass or metal bell minus its clapper.

### The Setup

Into one corner of the pocket handkerchief sew a curtain ring. A few stitches round the ring will ensure that it is securely attached to the surface of the material.

With the bell on the table, the performer is set to commence this somewhat unusual effect.

### Working and Presentation

In asking a spectator to assist, the performer selects one who wears a ring, requesting he or she to kindly loan it to him for the experiment to follow. The pocket handkerchief is removed from the performer's jacket and the ring is carefully placed underneath, so that it is in central position. In fact, the ring is placed over the index finger of the left hand, which at this point is under the handkerchief and out of view.

In removing the handkerchief, the corner, containing the secreted curtain ring, is handed to the spectator who grips his supposed finger ring through the folds of the material. The first finger of the left hand, containing the finger ring, is curled inward so that it is unseen.

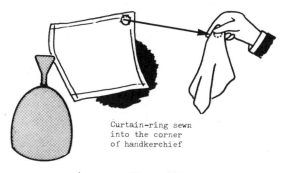

Curtain-ring sewn
into the corner
of handkerchief

**Figure 15.**

Meanwhile, the performer displays the bell in his right hand, drawing attention to the fact that it cannot ring.

The spectator's finger ring, secretly held on the first finger, is allowed to slide down into the palm of the hand where it is palmed. The bell is placed on top of the left palm and over the hidden ring.

"Sir, at this stage you are still holding your finger ring through the material of the pocket handkerchief . . . it is definitely there, isn't it? (the spectator admits this fact, for he can feel it through the handkerchief).

"I have been told that this particular bell will never ring again, but I cannot really believe this can be true. Perhaps, and only perhaps . . . tonight, a change will take place."

The performer retains hold of the handkerchief, snatches it away quickly so that the disappearance of the ring is apparent. The performer pockets the handkerchief.

With the spectator's finger ring now under the bell, the performer can dramatize the climax to the effect.

"One borrowed finger ring has vanished . . . into thin air, I may add, but perhaps for one simple reason. Perhaps this ring wishes to give life to a bell that cannot otherwise toll!"

Delivering these words, the performer is aware of a sudden ringing sound from within the bell. To make this sound possible, he has to merely rock his hand to and fro allowing the spectator's finger ring to come in contact with all sides of the bell.

"Yes, yes, there is a definite ring . . . can you hear it? Let's see what it can be," says the performer, as he lifts the bell from the hand.

And there inside is the spectator's own finger ring, making a startling appearance and ringing out to prove it has mysteriously arrived. It is ultimately handed to its rightful owner, who must surely verify its existence. It definitely has returned.


## PADLOCK RELEASE

An examined, locked padlock penetrates a length of rope of which both ends have been held securely by two assisting spectators.

### The Apparatus Required

Two small padlocks.
A length of rope.
A pocket handkerchief.

## The Setup

Thread one of the locked padlocks onto the length of rope so that it is positioned at one end. This rope is rested on top of the table with other items in front, so that it is not in view at this particular stage.

The second padlock, unlocked, is situated in the right jacket pocket alongside the key.

## Working and Presentation

The padlock is removed from the jacket pocket and handed to a spectator, who is requested to examine same. The key is handed to him so that he may lock the padlock, assuring everyone that it cannot possibly be opened. The spectator is asked to retain the key.

The performer displays the length of rope that is stretched between the hands, the right hand concealing the duplicate padlock, allowing the rope to run smoothly through the clenched fist, proving, for one, that it appears to be regular.

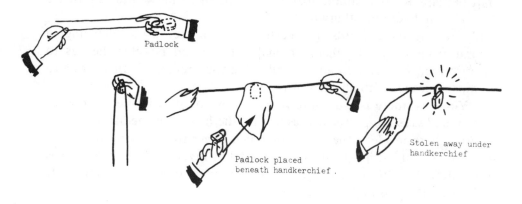

Padlock

Padlock placed
beneath handkerchief.

Stolen away under
handkerchief

**Figure 16.**

The performer's hand, concealing the duplicate padlock, is finally clenched around the center of the rope, both ends of which are visible. The left hand picks up the pocket handkerchief and drapes it over the fist. Two spectators assist by taking hold of the ends of the rope. The performer's right hand is casually removed as the rope is pulled taut. The duplicate padlock is now secretly positioned on the center of the rope.

The original padlock is displayed in the right hand, which then goes beneath the draped handkerchief. Undercover, the performer uses both hands to supposedly assist in making the padlock penetrate the rope, but in fact the right hand simply transfers the lock into the left. The left hand (concealing the lock) pulls away the handkerchief. Both handkerchief and padlock are casually pocketed. All eyes will be on the padlock, firmly threaded and secured to the center of the rope. It has to be unlocked to be released, should the spectators not wish to let go of their ends.

# 5 It Must Be Mind Reading

Do you believe in mind reading? I certainly do not, but then, that is just my opinion! Certainly we tricksters cannot claim any supernatural powers, for although we may be able to forecast the results of the football pools and predict the headlines of a newspaper a week in advance, we find it difficult to tell our public why we are not the wealthiest people living in the world.

The fact is that mental magic, as it is called, is trickery.

The performer who appears on your television screen, claiming powers that enable him to forecast, divine, and predict, is a conjurer playing the part of a mind reader. It is, therefore, not surprising that audiences actually believe his words and actions to be true.

If the student wishes to embark upon this very fascinating branch of the art, mentalism, he should follow the rules and codes that are laid down and that others, who have made their name, have followed successfully.

The performer should appear immaculately dressed. Costumes of a comedy nature are obviously not suitable for such a presentation.

The tricks should be referred to as experiments throughout. If any should go wrong, one can blame the experiment not being one hundred percent foolproof or that it is in its preliminary stages.

Patter should be concise, void of funny remarks, unless one can enhance a particular effect, and the performer's diction should be clear and understandable. A dramatic, powerful voice is what is required.

The student is advised to avoid mixing visual magic with mental tricks and routines. The two never seem to go together in the same program.

Never underestimate your audience's intelligence. Intelligent people as they are, they often become irritated by normal human beings claiming supernatural powers and offering challenges, backed by thousands of dollars. One well-known professional mentalist did just that some years ago and lost his entire savings.

Mental magic is designed to intrigue, stimulate the imagination, and entertain. Happy mind reading!

## FILLING THE BILL

From a choice of three envelopes, one containing a twenty dollar bill, the other two, messages, two spectators assist in selecting one each. However, the remaining one, retained by the performer, always contains the bill. A puzzling mental routine if ever there was one.

### The Apparatus Required

Three pay envelopes.
Three specially made message cards.
A twenty dollar bill.
A small magnet.

### Preparation

All three message cards are faked. Being double, two similar-sized pieces of thin card are glued together with a razor blade secreted between.

Messages, such as HARD LUCK!, BETTER LUCK NEXT TIME,

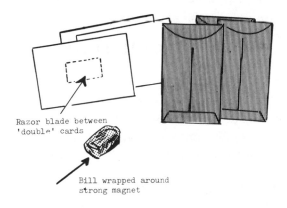

Razor blade between
'double' cards

Bill wrapped around
strong magnet

**Figure 17.**

SORRY—NO CHANCE!, are boldly marked upon the surfaces of the cards.

Wrap the twenty dollar bill around the magnet so that it becomes a neat package that can be concealed within the hands.

Place one of the message cards in each envelope. Conceal the bill in the right hand.

### Working and Presentation

Fanned in the right hand, all three envelopes are displayed to the audience. Request a spectator to select one envelope and remove this, handing it to him. Offer a second spectator the choice of the remaining two and emphasize that a change of mind is possible, even at this stage. Whichever envelope he or she selects, this is handed over. With the remaining envelope held in the hand, it is an easy matter for the performer to work up the bill, containing the magnet, behind this, where it will adhere to the razor blade within the message card, through the surface of the paper. At this stage both hands act freely in opening the envelope, the top being ripped open. The fingers of the right hand are seen to come over the front, the thumb actually entering inside, at the same time sliding up the bill so that it nears the palm position. The movement is presented quickly, so that the bill appears to come from the inside of the envelope and not from the back, where in fact it comes from.

So in effect, no matter which envelope remains, this procedure is adopted. A possible change of mind can be offered during the experiment. The message card contained within the third and final envelope is left inside.

The performer's envelope always contains the twenty dollar bill.

### TELEVISION TELEPATHY

This is a cute close-up mental routine.

A spectator is asked to write the name of his favorite television program within the screen area of the illustrated television set, which is boldly printed or drawn onto a square of paper. The spectator is also requested to fold this in half, and in half again, until it becomes a neat, folded packet.

The performer immediately tears the folded paper into many pieces, burning these in an nearby ashtray.

Moments later he is able to successfuly divulge the contents of the paper, divining the television program title that the spectator has selected.

## The Apparatus Required

A piece of paper measuring some 4" square.

With a felt-tipped pen, draw a bold outline of a television set, so that the screen area is positioned in the center.

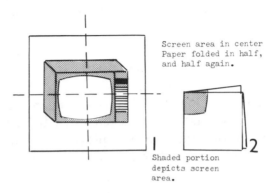

Screen area in center
Paper folded in half,
and half again.

Shaded portion
depicts screen
area.

**Figure 18.**

## Working and Presentation

To accomplish this little miracle, one must perform the classic "center tear" move, which is both effective and simple to do.

After the spectator has written the name of his favorite television program within the screen area of the illustration, request him to fold it in half.

Ask him to make a further fold.

The screen area, containing the vital information forms the central folds of the paper square. The shaded portion shows this clearly.

Taking the folded paper from the spectator, the performer commences to tear it into several pieces. The portion containing the information is separated from the other bits and ultimately gripped under the thumb, while the remainder is torn. In transferring all but this vital piece from right to left hand, the performer conceals it within the right. This hand casually goes to the jacket pocket and removes a box of matches, leaving behind this folded portion.

A match is struck, setting fire to the torn pieces in view, these being allowed to drop into the ashtray. While these burn, the right hand enters the jacket pocket to discard the matchbox, at the same time retaining the folded portion, concealing this within the hand and finally opening it out so that it is gripped in the cupped position of the hand. At this point, the information within the screen area can be glanced at and remembered.

Moving away from the ashtray containing ashes, the performer cups both hands around his forehead.

In revealing the chosen program, the performer answers carefully, "I see, by your thoughts, sir, that you are deeply interested in quiz games, and in particular, those which involve educational background. I can read from the ashes that your favorite television program is———!"

## TWIN THOUGHTS

Six important questions, boldly marked upon wooden blocks, are presented to any spectator who is requested to select just one. The performer divines the question and provides a suitable answer. The experiment can be immediately repeated.

### The Effect

Six wooden blocks, each bearing a different question marked on the tops, are displayed and handed to a member of the audience. A spectator is requested to select one of the blocks and then to place it inside a box, which holds it tightly, sealing it with the provided lid.

The performer immediately reveals knowledge of the question and answers it in a most accurate fashion.

### The Apparatus Required

Six wooden blocks, each bearing a different question, these being boldly marked on one side, assume a top position in this particular experiment.

The following questions could be used.

>SHALL I MARRY?
>SHALL I BECOME FAMOUS?
>WILL I PASS MAJOR EXAMS?
>SHALL I REMAIN HEALTHY?
>WILL I TRAVEL?
>SHALL I SUCCEED IN BUSINESS?

You also require a wooden or cardboard box large enough to hold one of the blocks. It is essential that there is a separate lid.

*Working and Presentation*

All six blocks are resting upon the performer's table so that the audience can see them clearly. Beside these is the box.

Requesting a spectator to select one of the blocks bearing the question of his choice, the performer places it into the box. With the question uppermost, the spectator himself handles the box and secures the lid on top. The box is then handed to the performer, who, during this procedure, has his back toward the audience. The remaining five visible blocks are removed and hidden.

Facing his audience now, the performer holds the box behind his back. A secret move takes place. The right hand quickly lifts up the lid, while the left hand gives the box a half-turn. The right hand replaces the lid on the new top position, bringing the box from behind his back so that it is in full view to the audience. Although the box appears as previously, from the back, the performer can glance at the question, for it visibly. Let us suppose the question is "WILL I TRAVEL?"

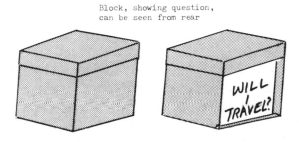

Block, showing question,
can be seen from rear

**Figure 19.**

"This box contains a question . . .,a question for answering, and answered it will be," says the performer, placing the box behind his back once more.

"Sir, you selected a very interesting question, one that I can confidently answer . . . YES! You are perhaps thinking of distant countries, new cities and towns to explore, and a *possible* chance to see the world. Through nature of your business you *may* travel in the near future. Certainly, if this should not be the case, there will be possibilities of travel on vacations."

Meanwhile, behind his back, the performer replaces the lid onto its proper place, brings the box to the front, and requests a spectator to open it and remove the block, revealing the question to everyone.

Replies to all six questions should be short and carefully worded.

Words such as "You may ... It could be possible ... Perhaps" are best used in such cases.

## NUMBER COMBINATION

Using the same principle as that of our previous effect, four numbered blocks and a box with a drop-on lid are used.

A spectator arranges the blocks in any combination he wishes, secures the lid, and hands the box to the performer, who ultimately divines the sequence by revealing the numbers one by one in rotation — a truly remarkable feat.

### *The Apparatus Required*

A shallow cardboard box made to hold four wooden blocks. It has a removable lid. Four wooden blocks. Each block numbered 1 to 4, with the six sides of each carrying its own number. Thus, the 2 block shows two's on all of its sides.

### *Working and Presentation*

No previous setting is required, and the blocks and box can be throughly examined before and after the effect.

Refer to the previous effect "Twin Thoughts" and duplicate the working and mechanics of the trick. Instead of one block, four are used, and the same "half-turn" move of the box is executed while it is held behind the back.

The spectator selects his number combination, placing the blocks, in sequence, into the box, and then closing the lid.

By executing the half-turn move the performer is able to glance at the blocks, which reveal enough of their surfances to allow him to remember these.

Here is a case of using the same principle to bring about a somewhat

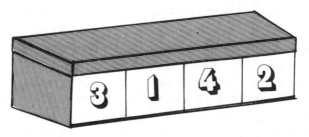

**Figure 20.**

different effect. Although, these methods are identical, the variation and adaptation warrant both being presented in the same program.

## MAGIC MARKERS

A novel mental routine using six different colored marker pens.

In performance, the pens are removed from a paper sack and displayed in the hand. All appear to look identical, but it is soon revealed that each tip is of a different color, the caps being removed to prove this fact.

Replacing the caps and arranging the pens so that it becomes impossible for anyone to know of the position of any one of the colors, a spectator is requested to select one, by simply pointing to it.

This particular pen is removed from the other five which are discarded inside the paper bag. In matter of seconds, the performer is able to reveal the color of the pen.

### The Apparatus Required

Twelve marker pens. Although six complete pens are required, twelve caps are needed, and it will be necessary to buy a double lot.

A paper sack.

### The Set-Up

Place the six extra caps onto the bottoms of each pen. The pens are carefully placed inside the paper sack so that the actual bottoms (with caps over these) go together.

### Working and Presentation

The right hand removes the pens from the sack. Gripping and concealing the duplicate caps in the hand, these ar displayed in an arc.

The left hand removes the visible caps showing that each tip is of a different color. Replacing these, he rearranges the pens, still concealing the duplicates at the opposite ends, so that it is impossible for anyone to know of the positions and colors.

Requesting a spectator to one of the pens, whichever is chosen, he carefully removes by the right hand, fingers cupping the bottom so to conceal the additional cap. The remaining five are discarded into the paper sack. As these are being placed inside, the pen, held in the right hand, is secretly reversed so that the bottom, containing the extra cap,

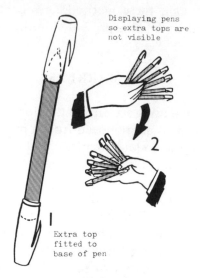

Displaying pens
so extra tops are
not visible

2

Extra top
fitted to
base of pen

**Figure 21.**

is in view. To all intents and puposes, it appears as before.

One simple move assists the performer in revealing the color of the pen.

Gripped between the thumb and fingers, the thumb pushes down on the cap, allowing it to snap off and fall into the awaiting curled fingers. A glance at the colored tip gives the performer all the information he requires.

The cap is quickly replaced, being forced back onto its end. While revealing the color of the pen, both hands come together to remove the uppermost cap so as to prove that the divination is correct. In fact, the pen is pivoted, under cover of the cupped hands, so that the colored tip is now in top position. The extra cap is now slid off the opposite end and left behind in the right hand.

The chosen pen can be handed to the spectator for thorough examination.

### A MATTER OF COLOR

Four slates, each of which displays a written color, RED, YELLOW, BLUE, and GREEN, are displayed to the audience.

These are well mixed, and one slate is chosen and placed inside a cloth bag. The performer holds this behind his back while he selects one of four differently colored pieces of card, all matching the colors on the slates.

The selected piece of card is dropped inside the bag alongside the chosen slate.

When the spectator is handed the slate it is seen to be marked on one side "YOU WILL SELECT RED" in red chalk, while the card, placed there by the performer, is red in color. A fantastic prediction!

### The Apparatus Required

Four school slates. Four flaps that fit inside the frames of the slates. Black in color and made in stout card of thin plastic, these become part of the slates when inserted.

On the front of each slate is written in chalk of a matching color. RED, YELLOW, GREEN, and BLUE. On the reverse sides is written "YOU WILL SELECT THIS COLOR".

The flaps are inserted inside the frames of the slates and on their surfaces is boldly marked the word "NO."

Trapped between each flap and slate is a piece of card, the color of which matches the one boldly marked on the slate surface.

You also require six cloth bags.

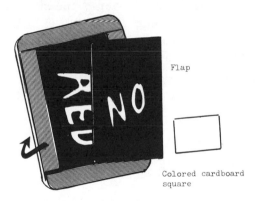

Figure 22.

### Working and presentation

The four slates are displayed showing the different colors written in chalk. The slates are mixed, so that the audience is not aware of their positions, and the performer must be careful in handling the slates, assuring that the flaps remain within the frames.

The six cloth bags are proved empty by being turned inside out.

The slates are placed inside their individual bags and lined upon the table. In doing so, the performer makes a point of dislodging the flap within each frame, allowing it to drop away and fall to the bottom of the bag.

While the performer turns his back, away from the audience a spectator is asked to select one bag and then carefully hand it over.

Held behind his back, the performer further displays six pieces of colored cards, those matching the ones marked upon the slates surfaces. The performer selects one at random, so that no one can possibly see its face, and explains that he intends placing it inside the bag alongside the slate. What in fact happens is that the card is secretly pocketed or placed up the sleeve. The remaining five cards are openly discarded in the trouser pocket out of view.

Recapping to the audience, the performer explains that from six slates, each marked with a different color was chosen by the performer and then dropped into the selected bag, containing the slate.

When the bag is brought to the front, it is opened. The slate is removed leaving the flap behind. This in turn has dislodged the planted piece of card, bearing an identical color.

First, the performer displays the color markings on the face of the slate. Second, he reaches inside the bag removing the card that is seen to match color. Finally, he reverses the slate revealing that the opposite side carries the wording "YOU WILL SELECT ———"

The remaining five slates can be carefully removed from their bags so that the flap is still within each frame and all can be shown to display the word "NO."

# 6 Now You See It— Now You Don't
# (Simple Lessons on Sleight-of-Hand)

What is sleight-of-hand?

I have often heard the layman say that such dexterity relies upon the quickness of the hand deceiving the eye, but I personally disagree with that viewpoint.

Sleight-of-hand is magic pure and simple — magic using everyday objects, mainly involving the hands.

Much enjoyment can be had from learning the various moves and manipulations that are described in this chapter. These have been evolved over thousands of years and to this day are in constant use, used by the professional and amateur alike.

Should the student solely be interested in presenting conjuring with apparatus, a basic knowledge of sleight-of-hand is still essential. By knowing and then putting to practice such moves, one can often overcome uncertain mishaps that undoubtedly can occur during a performance. It is possible, then, to inject an improptu, unplanned sleight-of-hand move into a sequence that has failed to register.

In presenting sleight-of-hand, the student is advised to pay particular attention to hand care, and, in particular, to the neatness of the fingernails. These are always on view, normally at close quarters and under minute observation. It is essential that the hands are clean, fingernails neatly trimmed, and that shirt cuffs are spotlessly laundered.

Numerous action photographs, designed in a step-by-step fashion, assist the student in becoming familiar with the basic and more ad-avanced sleight-of-hand techniques. If practicing these in front of a mirror, the student is reminded that hand positions appear in reverse.

I am sure the readers will find this particular branch of magic slightly mysterious, to say the least.

## BILLIARD BALL MANIPULATIONS

The turn of the century saw the start of specialization. With cards, there was Howard Thurston; with coins, Nelson Downs; Stilwell with handkerchiefs; and Fowler with watches.

While De Kolta had added a new dimension to the production of balls resembling those used for the game of billiards, it was a Danish magician, Clement de Lion, who decided to make a specialty using these objects. In Britain a young magician whose life was to be short indeed, Martin Chapender, though not confining himself to these objects in his impeccable manipulative act, did, using full-sized ivory billiard balls, attain a state of perfection unequaled by any other manipulative magician of that time.

The trick, that of producing a number of billiard balls at the fingertips, became a stable part of the magical repertory, often there being little additions well shown in David Devant's "Multiplication," so well described in the classic book *Our Magic*. Devant made the strong point that so much depended upon the use of real ivory balls.

In the hands of the expert it could be a great trick, while in lesser accomplished performers it was something to arouse mild interest. Nevertheless it stayed, and in the thirties one saw the trick become a feat of real magic in the hands of that great Welsh magician Cardini, while in the Antipodes, Maurice Rooklyn, with incredible dexterity, once again had a specialized act using these commonplace objects.

Alongside such professionals at that time was Brian McCarthy, an outstanding amateur, whose production and color changes made his superb performance one never to be forgotten.

In the past two decades magicians have seen the trick taken further, so that the performer, not content at producing the standard four balls at the fingertips, excelled by materializing some fourteen, all of which were firmly and carefully held in the hands. Two such great exponents achieving this feat are English-born manipulators, Ron McMillan and Geoffrey Buckingham.

### Palming a Ball

Crutch of the thumb grips the ball tightly so that the hand can almost appear fully opened (see Plate 1).

### Finger-Palm

Curled finger keeps the ball secreted in this position.
Front view (see Plate 2).
Back view (see Plate 3).

*Plate* 1. Palm position.

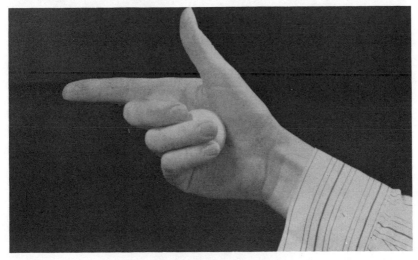

*Plate* 2. Curled finger retains ball.

93

## Showing Both Hands Empty

Should the occasion arise when the performer wishes to show *both* hands empty and then produce a ball, this following method is most suitable and convincing.

The first finger of the right hand points to the left hand, emphasizing that it is empty (the concealed ball is finger-palmed in the right hand) (see Plate 3).

Both hands are clenched as fists (the ball still remains within the right hand) (see Plate 4). The right hand fist overlaps the left.

The concealed ball is allowed to "roll" over the back of the left hand as the right hand is fully opened for display purposes. (For rear view, see Plate 5).

From the front, both hands look convincingly empty. The ball, in fact, is hidden behind the hands, with the right-hand thumb holding pressure against it (see Plate 6), the perfect method of showing both hands empty.

A reverse procedure is required to obtain the ball back into the right hand, so that it is again concealed within the palm. From this position, a sudden production can be made.

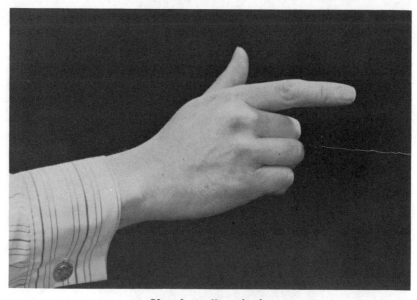

*Plate* 3. Audience's view.

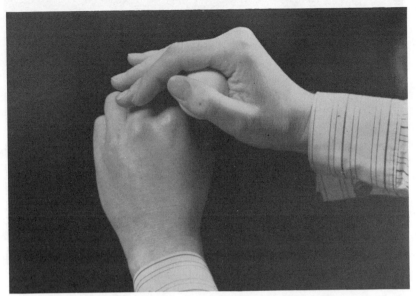

*Plate* 4. Right hand approaches left, ball concealed.

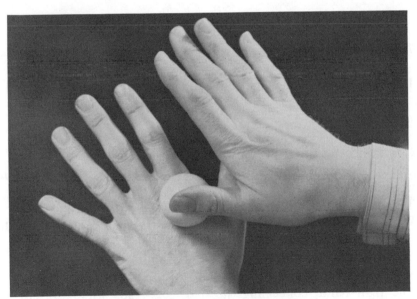

*Plate* 5. Hidden ball rolls over back of hand.

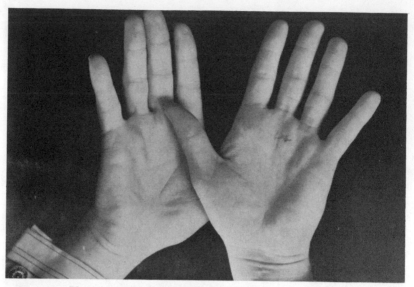

*Plate* 6. Audience's view: hands appear to be empty.

### Billiard Ball Sequence

Use several moves, sleights, and standard manipulations.

### Change-over Palm

Commence by finger-palming the ball in the left hand. The ball can be easily gripped in this position from the jacket pocket where it is secretly held (see Plate 7).

The right hand is shown to be empty. It comes toward the left.

With the left hand now above the right, the ball is allowed to drop from its upper position into the awaiting hand beneath (see Plate 8). During this move, a quick right turn of the body is required so that the execution is not suspected by members of the audience.

The right hand, concealing the ball, gets ready for the production. The thumb forces the ball up on top of the clenched fist (see Plate 9).

The change-over palm has been successfully executed. Apparently, both hands have been shown empty. In effect, you have transferred a secreted ball from one hand to the other, resulting in actually producing a billiard ball on top of the fist.

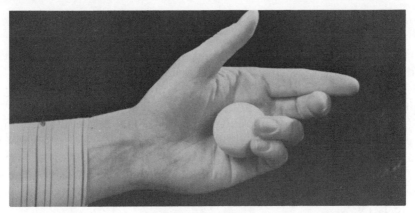

*Plate* 7. Ball finger-palmed.

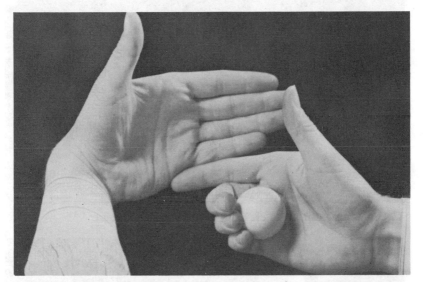

*Plate* 8. Right hand approaches, ball is dropped from left.

*Plate* 9. Thumb assists in forcing ball onto fist.

97

With the ball in the last mentioned position, the left hand is placed in front of the ball (see Plate 10).

The fingers of this hand are closed, supposedly surrounding the ball, in the act of removing it from this position.

The ball, in fact, drops into the right hand, as the left hand, pretending to hold it, comes away, as though gripping it firmly (see Plate 11).

The right hand, finger-palming the ball, points to the left hand with the fist finger. The left hand is fully opened to show the vanish (see Plate 12).

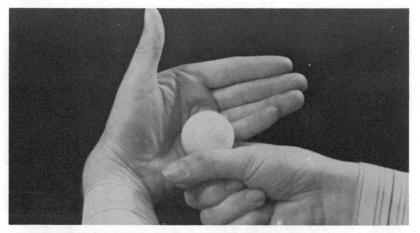

*Plate* 10. **Left hand covers ball (back view).**

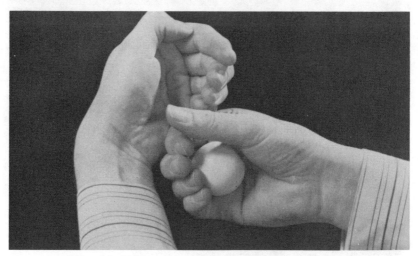

*Plate* 11. **Making fist while ball drops into right hand.**

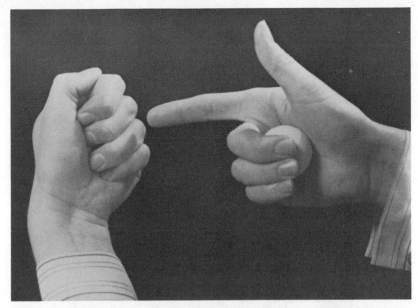

*Plate* 12. Right hand (concealing ball) points to left, supposedly containing same.

### Continuation — A Production

With the ball still in the finger-palm position, the right hand reaches behind the sleeve of the jacket and produces it from the elbow.

### Throw-Up Vanish

The ball, at this stage resting on the palm of the right hand, is thrown into the air and then caught between the hands. The flourish is repeated to establish this fact. However, upon executing the flourish a third time, the ball is not thrown. The left hand comes forward to assist in the catch (see Plate 13).

While the left hand pretends to hold the ball, the right, concealing the palmed ball, points (see Plate 14).

Slowly, the fingers of the left hand open singly to reveal the sudden vanish of the ball. The ball, at this stage, is concealed in the right hand palm position.

It is reproduced by release pressure of the fingers and thumb, bringing it up into view, and ultimately resting on top of the closed fist.

99

*Plate* 13. Ball thrown from left hand to right.

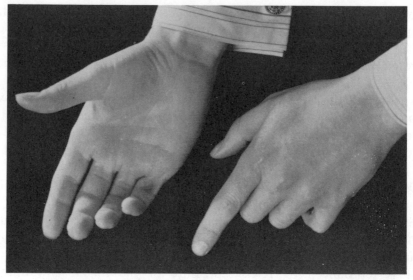

*Plate* 14. In action, right "catches" it, but it is retained in left.

While the right hand displays the same ball, between finger and thumb position, the left forms a fist (see Plate 15).

The ball is forced into the first (see Plate 16).

The thumb of the right hand assists in pushing it in further.

In executing this "poking" move the ball is allowed to drop through the opening so as to fall into the awaiting left hand. (For the performer's view, see Plate 17.)

In removing the thumb, the right hand comes away with the ball now nicely concealed within the curled finger (see Plate 18).

The first finger of the right hand further pushes in the supposed ball.

The vanish, as seen by the audience: the left hand is opened to show that it is empty (see Plate 19).

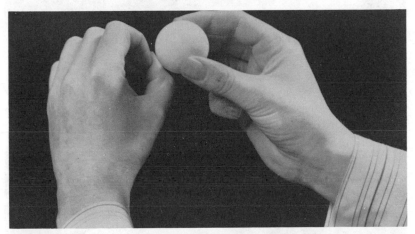

*Plate* 15. Right hand approaches left with ball.

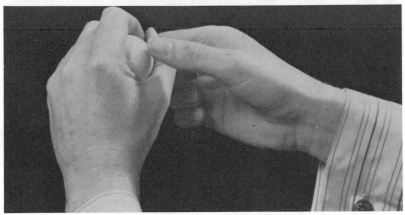

*Plate* 16. Ball being forced into left fist.

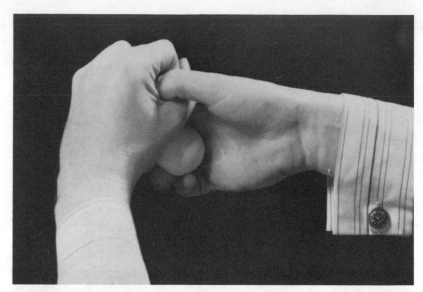

*Plate* 17. In poking ball, thumb allows it to drop into waiting right hand.

*Plate* 18. Right hand, concealing ball, points to closed fist.

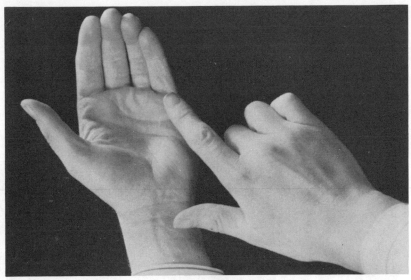

*Plate* 19. The vanish. Left hand is opened.

### The Final Reproduction

Continuing from the above position, the right hand nears the left, secretly plants the hidden ball against the palm of the hand, and rolls it downward so that it makes a sudden and lasting appearance.

The sequence described covers many aspects in the field of ball manipulation. Productions, vanishes and transpositions have been covered admirably in such a short period of time. Although such moves and sleights can be performed individually, these have been designed to blend into the sequence that has been presented. One step follows another, blending into a splendid routine of manipulations.

### Color-changing Ball

Should the student wish to include a nifty color change of a billiard ball into his act, this following method, although relying upon sleight-of-hand, can provide the solution.

You require two balls, one white, one red.

The white ball is concealed in the left hand, finger-palmed, while the right displays a red ball, this resting on top of the fist.

The left hand nears forward the right, covering the red ball (see Plate 20).

Still concealing the white ball within the left hand, this hand now pretends to take away the red, by making a clutching motion. In fact, while this is being done, the red ball is allowed to drop into the right hand (see Plate 21).

The left hand, now holding the white ball, moves away from the right hand, which finger-palms the red ball. (for rear view, see Plate 22.)

Upon opening the hand, the ball is seen to have changed color. The white ball is now displayed — a miraculous change indeed!

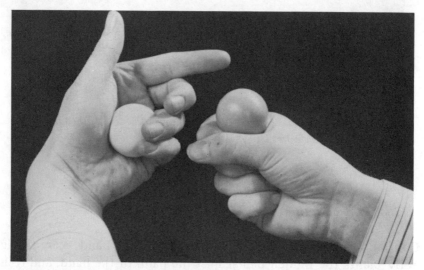

*Plate* 20. Left hand, containing white ball, approaches right, similarly palming a ball (red).

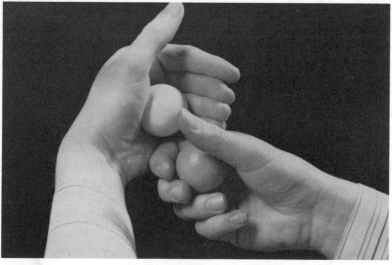

*Plate* 21. Left hand supposedly removes the red ball from the fist, but this ball drops into palm position.

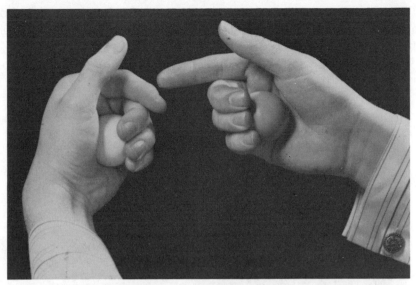

*Plate* 22. **Right hand points to left. The color change has been made.**

## CARD MANIPULATIONS

The manipulation of playing cards, so that the pasteboards appear, reappear, vanish, and transpose, sounds interesting and is something that the beginner perhaps longs to accomplish. However, much practice is required in the execution of the various moves that enable the performer to perform such feats.

The student is asked to study the various aspects of card manipulation before embarking upon actually presenting a sequence before the public.

### Vanishing a Playing Card

The right hand removes a card from the pack, holding this between the first finger and thumb (see Plate 23).

As the throwing motion is made, the thumb pivots back the card, while the little finger is positioned toward the bottom edge of the card (see Plate 24).

With the first finger gripping the upper edge of the card and the little finger curling inward to secure it, the pivoting move is made (see Plate 25).

Plate 26 shows a side view of how the card is actually pivoted back into "back-palm" position.

The front view photograph shows how the hand can be shown empty. The edges of the cards are visible here, through the fingers. (Slightly exaggerated here to prove the point).

The card can be reproduced using reverse procedure, it being pivoted forward so that it appears between the fingers.

*Plate* 23. **Card held between thumb and fingers.**

*Plate* 24. **Little and first fingers curl inward.**

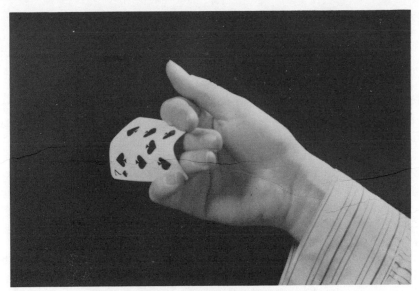

*Plate* 25. Card is allowed to curl backward.

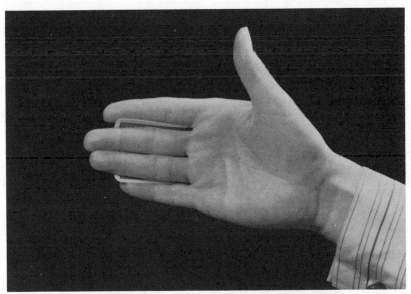

*Plate* 26. Front view: Exaggerated card edges.

Now that the student is familiar with the vanishing and reproduction methods used by manipulators using a single card, let us now consider the possibility of repeat card productions.

So far, we have learned about the front- and back-palming techniques, which are responsible for most of the manipulations conjurers use.

The same procedure is adopted in the production of numerous cards, except that instead of one card being manipulated, a "stock" of cards (i.e., ten to twelve cards) is secured between the first and third fingers.

Cards held in this position are ready to be produced, allowing the fingers to curl inward so that the thumb presses against the corners of the cards (see Plate 27).

The thumb pushes the top card upward and away from the others, while the little finger releases tension. The card comes free from the others, appearing between the fingertips.

Discarded into a hat or suitable container, the following card is produced in similar fashion. All of the cards are produced in this manner.

*Plate* 27. **Thumb peels off single cards from stack.**

## Cheeky Production

Continuing the production, until the last card remains between the fingertips, the performer can produce numerous cards by using a somewhat cheeky move.

The single card is gripped between the fingers and ready for the vanish move. The card is supposedly dropped inside the hat, but undercover, is pivoted into back-palm position, ready for a further production. The hand can be shown empty each time it is withdrawn from the hat or container and can produce as many cards as you feel adequate enough to achieve good results.

## Production of Fans of Cards

Now that we have discussed how to produce cards singly, let us examine the possibilities of producing fans, one after another. The principle used is the same, except that instead of one card being back-palmed, a stock of cards is held in this position.

The student is advised to try a few cards at first, adding to these as he progresses. Some performers, being completely skillful, have been known to back-palm almost half a deck!

The stock of cards can be stolen from behind a hat or container, these being gripped in back-palm position. Alternatively, these can be

*Plate* 28. **Finger-breaking a number of cards.**

*Plate* 29. **Cards being brought into back-palm position.**

stolen from the jacket pocket, the cards being firmly gripped in the same position.

A fan of cards is produced in the same manner as in the production of one, these being pivoted from the back-palm position. The cards come to view, are fanned, and are displayed to the audience.

In discarding what supposedly looks like the complete fan, the first finger of the right hand makes a definite break, only some four or five cards down from the top of the stock (see Plate 28).

Both first and little fingers engage into the back-palm position ready to pivot back the remaining cards while the few cards are thrown into the hat or container (see Plate 29).

The same back-palmed cards are produced in a further fan, and again, after a break has been made, only a few are allowed to drop from the hand. This procedure is repeated until all cards are exhausted. The final presentable fan is discarded into the hat.

### Productions of Cards from the Front of the Hand

This method varies from that of the back-palm hand position. In performance, the back of the hand faces the audience, and the cards are produced singly, materializing at the fingertips.

The student is advised to use six cards at first, these being plamed.

The thumb pushes against the outer corner of the stock of cards (see Plate 30).

The card is controlled between the first and second fingers (see Plate 31).

Continuing the movement, the card is now pivoted over (see Plate 32).

The rear view shows how the first of several cards is produced (see Plate 33).

The cards are repeatedly pivoted so as to appear in this display position.

*Plate* 30. Stack of cards palmed, thumb resting on top

*Plate* 31. Thumb pushes card away from top position.

111

*Plate* 32. Thumb goes beneath card to pivot it over.

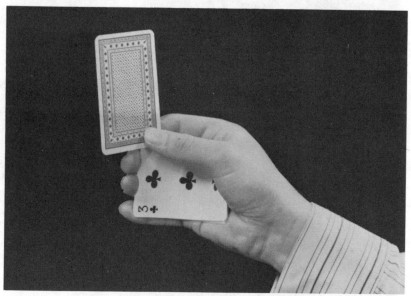

*Plate* 33. Pivoted card now in position for production. Remainder of stack concealed.

112

# SLEIGHT-OF-HAND WITH CIGARETTES

In reminiscing, I can recall the fabulous act of master manipulators such as Keith Clark, a European, living in America for most of his lifetime. As an authority on cigarette manipulation, he was responsible for the publication of the *Encyclopedia of Cigarette Tricks.*

As far back as 1905, Zirka, the queen of smokers, presented her most beautiful act in the Casino de Paris, proving that it was not solely male performers who were capable of such manipulations.

Frakson, the man with a hundred cigarettes, proved successful in South America, presenting manipulations that were acclaimed as being the simplest yet most direct in their nature.

In Britain was the name of Deveen, a skilled manipulator, whose manual "Expert Cigarette Manipulations" helped many a student on the road to success.

In the sixties British magician David Berglas scored heavily by producing endless streams of cigarettes while his shirt sleeves were rolled up to his elbows.

South African-born illusionist Robert Harbin must have entertained tens of thousands with his famous cigarette interlude in which a lighted cigarette repeatedly vanished from his lips only to reappear in the same position each time.

## Palming Cigarettes

There are several methods of palming lighted and unlighted cigarettes. Here are a few of the most practical versions.

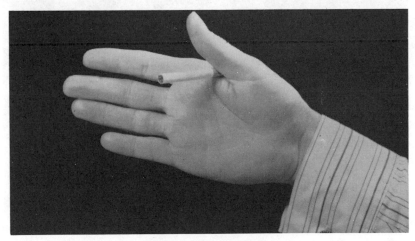

*Plate* 34. The position.

## Thumb Palm

The cigarette (lighted or unlighted) is gripped between the fleshy part of the thumb and first finger. It is held at an angle so that from the front, it cannot be seen (see Plate 34).

In producing it from this position, the first two fingers of the hand bend inward, grip the cigarette, and bring it out, so that it appears between the fingers as in Plate 35.

## Palming Five Cigarettes

It is possible for five cigarettes to be palmed in the same, above-mentioned manner.

The cigarettes are firmly gripped in a line, these angling inwards (see Plate 36).

Once they are secreted in this position, the student will find, after some practice, that it is possible to produce them singly, discarding each before the next is plucked from thin air. The first two fingers, as in thumb-palm, bend inward to pivot out the cigarettes. A smooth flourish, of reaching into the air or toward various parts of one's body, makes each production appear different and unusual.

However, one must first plan a method of obtaining the five cigarettes in this position, quickly and easily without suspicion.

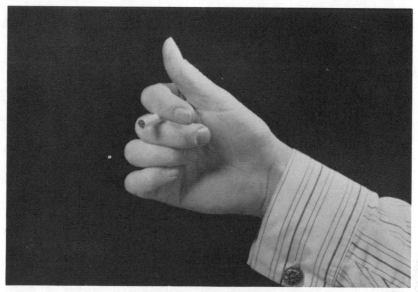

**Plate 35.** First and second fingers curl inward to grip cigarette, for production.

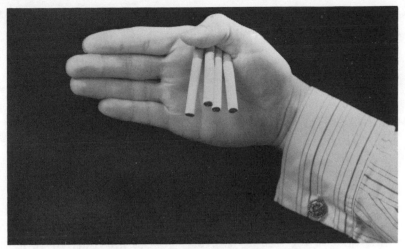

*Plate* 36. Cigarettes in thumb-palm position.

### Faked Cigarette Packet

A simple yet effective method of obtaining the required cigarettes in the finger-grip position is to fake a regular cigarette packet so that it does the work for you.

A flip-top pack is required, and from it, the base is removed. Using a piece cut from a wide elastic band, or a strip of flat elastic, this is attached, by the aid of a desk stapler, to the inside panel (see fig. 23). Six cigarettes can be secured behind this strip. Five of the six cigarettes are made to protrude a half an inch or more from the base.

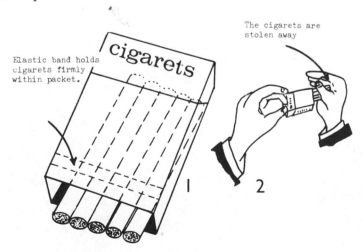

Elastic band holds
cigarets firmly
within packet.

*cigarets*

The cigarets are
stolen away

1

2

**Figure 23.**

115

The packet containing the cigarettes can already be positioned within the pocket or can be lying upon a table, ready for pick-up.

*The Working*

Upon removing the packet from his pocket, the performer takes particular care in not revealing the protruding cigarettes by covering these with the fingers of the right hand. The packet is gripped by the base, the tips of the cigarettes resting against the fleshy part of the thumb and first finger. As the packet is drawn away in a downward fashion the cigarettes are secretly gripped in this position. Even while gripping the cigarettes like this, both the thumb and finger can assist in reaching inside the packet to remove the remaining one. This cigarette is slid out of the elastic strip, the packet now being discarded. The performer places the visible cigarette to his lips but, in reflection, decides to discard it into the hat.

The moment it drops from the fingers the first and second fingers act quickly by bending inward, producing each cigarette individually. All five cigarettes are produced in this manner and are then discarded into the hat.

### Vanishing a Cigarette

Here is a practical way to vanish a cigarette.
Display the cigarette in the right hand.
Place it into the clenched fist (see Plate 37).
The right-hand thumb continues to push it inside (see Plate 38).
In doing so, it emerges from the other end (see Plate 39).
The middle fingers of the right hand now secretly grip the protruding cigarette, stealing it away.
The right hand, concealing the cigarette, points toward the left-hand clenched fist, which assumingly contains the cigarette (see Plate 40).
The vanish: the hand is opened while the right hand reproduces the palmed cigarette.

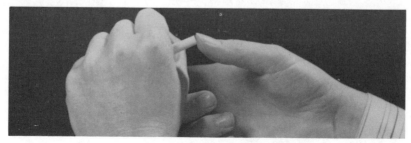

*Plate* 37. **Left hand pushes cigarette into fist.**

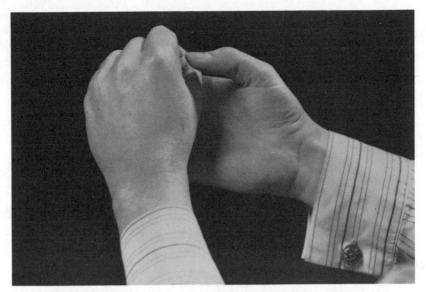

*Plate* 38. Nearing to right fist, left forces cigarette inside.

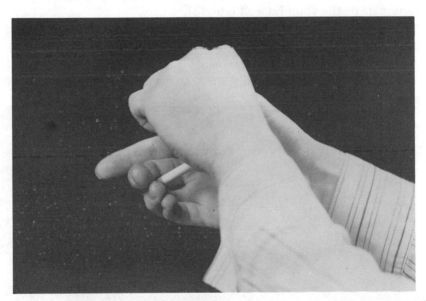

*Plate* 39. Cigarette seen to actually enter left hand, being gripped between middle fingers.

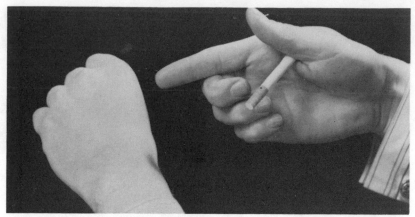

*Plate* 40. Cigarette retained in thumb-palm position, ready for the vanish.

### Another Vanish

The action of placing a cigarette into an awaiting hand is a natural one, and, in this particular version, simplicity is the keynote.

The right hand holds the cigarette between the first two fingers while the left hand is shown empty (see Plate 41).

As the right hand begins to "place" the cigarette into the left, both fingers bend inward so that the tip of the cigarette is gripped by the fleshy part of the thumb (see Plate 42).

The left-hand fingers cup as the right hand is withdrawn, giving the impression that the cigarette has been left behind.

Plate 43 shows the rear view, the cigarette in thumb-palm position.

The vanish: fingers gradually open to reveal that the hand is empty.

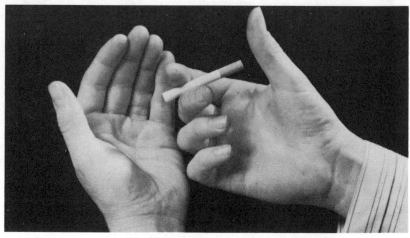

*Plate* 41. Cigarette displayed in right hand.

*Plate* 42. Supposedly being placed into left, cigarette is retained in right hand.

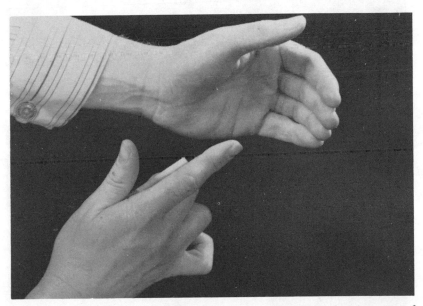

*Plate* 43. Left hand opens to show vanish. Exaggerated photo showing concealed cigarette.

### Reproduction of the Cigarette

With the cigarette in the above-mentioned position, the performer is able to put it to his advantage, involving yet further moves so that the cigarette can be reproduced (see Plate 43).

Reverse the left hand, right-hand index finger still pointing (see Plate 44).

The right hand draws nearer to the left, and on top.

Both hands are swiftly swung around so that they appear to be empty.

Back view: The concealed cigarette in thumb-palm (see Plate 45).

The right hand swings back so that the cigarette is in its original position.

Production of the cigarette is made.

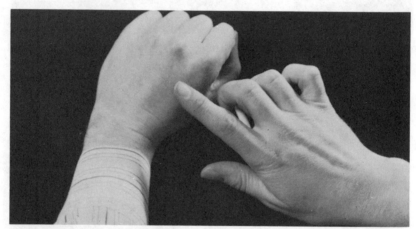

*Plate* 44. **Right hand nears left.**

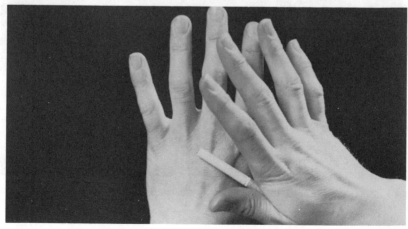

*Plate* 45. **Cigarette concealed behind hands (back view).**

## A Sliding Vanish

A cigarette, slid into the left fist, suddenly vanishes.

The cigarette is held between the index finger and thumb of the right hand (see Plate 46).

When the performer pushes it into the left fist, only the top of the cigarette enters, and the first finger slides up the length of the cigarette, which, viewed by the front, appears to give the impression that it is now inside (see Plate 47).

The cigarette is now concealed behind the curled first finger, which then points toward the empty left hand (see Plate 48).

The reproduction of the cigarette comes easily as the thumb and second finger, gripping it tightly, pivot it outward so as to make its appearance.

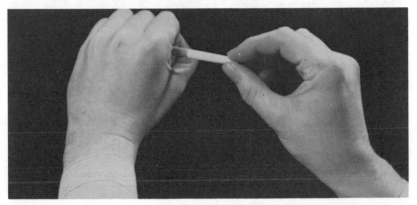

*Plate* 46. Right hand commences to push cigarette into fist.

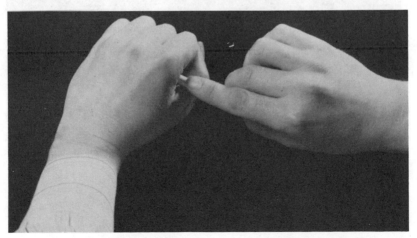

*Plate* 47. First finger slides along, appearing to push it inside.

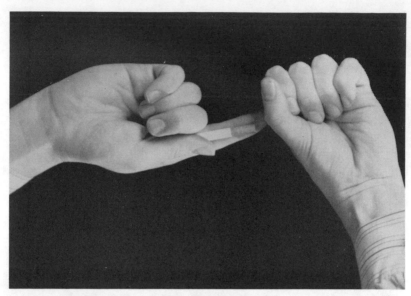

*Plate* 48. Back view.

### Back-Palming Cigarettes

The cigarette is gripped between the first and third fingers, actually lying against the second finger.

For a back view of the palmed cigarette, see Plate 49.

For a front view, as the audience sees the hand, see Plate 50.

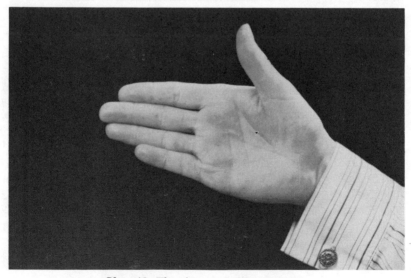

*Plate* 49. The view as audience sees it.

## Vanishing a Lighted Cigarette

The simple vanish of a lighted cigarette: one moment it is inside the hand, the next, it has vanished completely, only to reappear seconds later.

Hold a lighted cigarette between the first and second fingers of the right hand, with approximately a quarter of an inch of the lighted end protruding. The opposite end of the cigarette rests on the pad of the thumb (see Plate 51).

The right hand comes toward the cupped left hand.

The secret move. The cigarette, gripped between the first and second fingers, is brought into thumb-palm position (see Plate 52).

The closed left hand supposedly contains the cigarette. Note that the right hand conceals the cigarette while the first finger points to the left.

The left hand is opened to display the vanish, while the right reproduces the cigarette (see Plate 53).

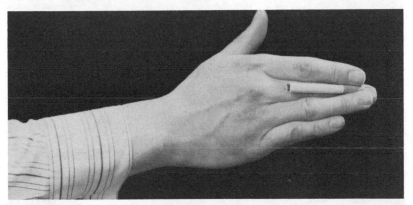

*Plate* 50. Back view showing cigarette gripped between first and third fingers.

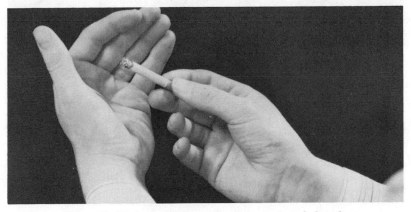

*Plate* 51. Right hand places lit cigarette into left palm.

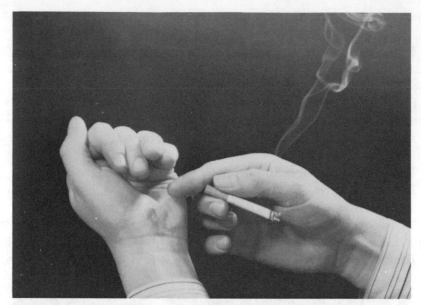

*Plate* 52. Cigarette is pivoted back into right.

*Plate* 53. Reproduction of lit cigarette from right hand.

# THIMBLE MANIPULATIONS

Although the thimble is a commodity that is solely associated with the home, it plays an important part in the work of the magician.

Because the thimble fits neatly over the finger, many sleights and moves are possible, allowing the performer to use such a commodity to his advantage.

The most cunning of thimble manipulators, to my mind, was the late John Ramsay. Born in Ayr, Scotland, his thimbles, carrying his name and address, were always presented to members of the audience, and the thimbles have now become rare to collectors of magical items.

Whether the manipulator chooses thimbles made in metal or plastic, he still has to practice the various moves and sleights without unnecessary fumbling. Metal thimbles, in my opinion, are best used for manipulation, for the indentations on these assist the performer in better palming and handling.

## Back-Palming a Thimble

For a quick production of a thimble, this method is superb.

The thimble is gripped between the first and third fingers. For a back view, see Plate 54.

All fingers curl inward (see Plate 55).

The thumb enters the thimble (see Plate 56).

The production is shown in Plate 57.

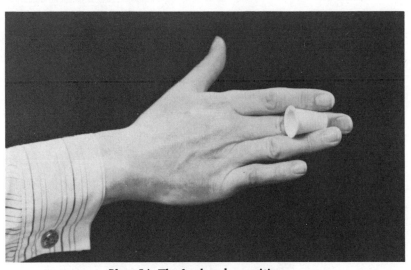

*Plate* 54. The back-palm position.

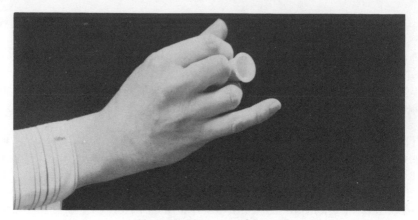

*Plate* 55. Fingers curl inward.

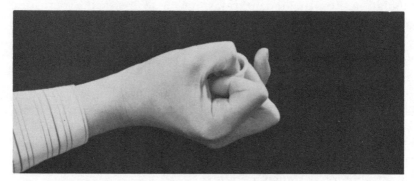

*Plate* 56. Thumb enters thimble.

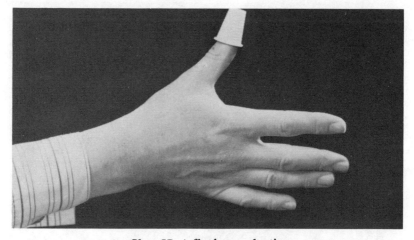

*Plate* 57. A final reproduction.

# 7 Novel Stage and Platform Tricks

The tricks that have been devised for this chapter have been solely designed for stage or platform use. Some, I have found, are suitable for cabarets, such as dinners, nightclubs, and functions that usually do not provide a platform or backcloth.

Here is magic using larger objects, those sometimes specially manufactured, but all within the capability of the reader to build and present: colorful conjuring, marvelous magic that can be presented to audiences large and small.

Presenting a stage or platform show demands careful and solid planning.

One should be particular in the items used, and these should be routined and presented in an ordinary fashion.

In providing a stage setting, the performer should supply his own form of table on which his apparatus will be displayed. A "roll-on"-type table or metal trolley is ideal, as too are those specially made collapsible side tables, produced and sold by magical dealers throughout the world.

Finally, should the student wish to make his debut on stage or platform, he should first learn stagecraft and showmanship techniques, makeup assembly, and, should patter enter into his act, elocution.

The stage is yours for the taking—made good use of it!

# RED OR BLUE?

A pack of cards, displaying blue backs, is removed from its case, fanned, and placed inside. The performer shows that the case also displays a similar blue-backed design card on its back.

He places his hand over this, and the display card suddenly changes color, to that of a red-backed card. Upon opening the case, and in removing the pack, the backs of these are now seen to be red in color.

## The Apparatus Required

Two decks of cards, each bearing a different colored back design. From both, remove twenty-six cards, placing these cards face to face so that one half of the deck can be fanned displaying red backs while the reverse side shows blues.

The card case is specially prepared in as much that the display card on the back panel (usual with most decks) can be made to change from blue to red by passing the hand over same. In fact, this consists of a flap card, made from two cards, one red and one blue backed. Figure 23 shows the construction. Both cards are scored and then folded in central positions. Stuck together with glue on the portions marked X, the remaining parts are glued onto the back panel of the case. When this flap is operated, one side displays the blue back design while the other shows red. One simple hand movement over the display card allows it to become red or blue when required.

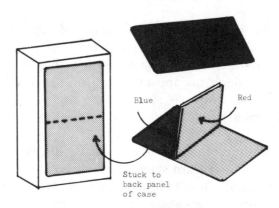

Blue            Red

Stuck to
back panel
of case

**Figure 24.**

## The Setup

The deck, set in the above-mentioned manner, is inside its case. The display card on the back panel of the case should be set to show a blue design.

## Working and Presentation

Remove the deck from its case. Fan the deck to the point where the cards become reversed, making the most of displaying half the pack as one, at this particular point. The audience clearly sees that the back designs are blue at this stage.

Replace the deck inside the case and draw attention toward the display card on its back. The fingers of the left hand assure that the upper portion of the flap is held firmly against the surface of the hinged card. In placing the right hand over the display card, it is pivoted downward, bringing the red design into view.

The deck is carefully removed from its case so that the red-backed cards are shown, these being fanned in a similar manner, stopping at the halfway mark where the reversed cards take over.

The sudden color change of the back designs comes as a surprise to the audience, especially after the display card on the back panel of the case has also changed.

Like most platform tricks, the specially made deck must never be left idle for spectators to examine. Here is one effect, in particular, where the performer should casually dispose of the properties quickly, and rapidly continue with others that follow naturally.

## EGG-XAGERATION!

An egg suddenly appears within an empty eggcup. The effect is quick, slick, and very visual.

### The Apparatus Required

A plastic eggcup.
A joke plastic or heavy rubber egg.
A length of heavy, yet almost invisible, thread.
A small, plastic bead.

## Preparation

With a hot needle or spike, bore or burn a hole through the base of the eggcup.

Similarly, burn two holes through the base of the plastic or rubber egg so that it is possible for a length of thread to be brought through, this being firmly secured.

Lead the thread through the base of the eggcup, through the hole in its base, and to its end, fasten the plastic bead.

Since the trick has been designed as an "opener," the setup is as follows.

With the length of thread fully extended, the egg is secretly placed under the left armpit. The bead protrudes slightly from underneath the cup, and the thumb and forefinger of the right hand now hold this without causing suspicion.

## Working and Presentation

The performer enters holding the eggcup in his right hand.

When he wishes the egg to appear inside the cup he (1) retains grip of the bead; (2) quickly pulls this so that the thread thightens, bringing out the egg from under the armpit, swiftly traveling so that it assumes a new position, that on top of the cup.

The maneuver must be executed both quickly and smoothly.

From the audience's point of view, the appearance of an egg inside its cup has taken place in a surprising manner.

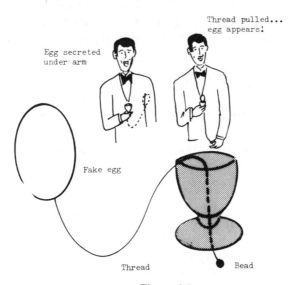

**Figure 25.**

130

# SWINGING BOTTLE

A soda, lemonade, vinegar, or indeed any clear glass bottle is mysteriously suspended on the end of a length of rope. Furthermore, the bottle is swung from side to side and then completely around. Both the bottle and length of rope are thoroughly examined before and after the effect.

## *The Apparatus Required*

A suitable clear bottle.
A glass or plastic ball.
A length of soft rope or silky cord.

## *Preparation*

The length of rope and glass ball are contained in the right jacket pocket.

The bottle (this can be a borrowed one) is nearby, ready to use.

## *Working and Presentation*

Pick up the bottle, displaying it, and remove the length of rope from the pocket, secretly concealing the glass ball within the hand at the same time.

Both bottle and rope are handed to a spectator for examination. When returned, the performer lowers one end of the rope inside the bottle. It is removed for a few moments, and, in fact, the performer is merely establishing the fact that the rope comes away freely.

In holding the neck of the bottle in the right hand, the glass ball is allowed to slowly roll and drop inside. It will be unnoticed at this stage of the trick, thanks to its transparency.

Once the end of the rope enters inside the bottle, it is an easy matter for the performer to invert the neck of the bottle so that it is now facing the floor. Immediately, the glass ball drops to the neck and lodges the rope against the side of the bottle. When the bottle is held high, the rope is seen to magically hang from it. Furthermore, because the rope is pulled taught, it is possible for the bottle to be swung first from side to side and then completely around, climaxing in a most startling magical effect.

In disengaging the clear ball from the neck of the bottle, the performer holds the mouth upward and lowers the rope slightly so that it becomes free. The length of rope is carefully removed, being handed

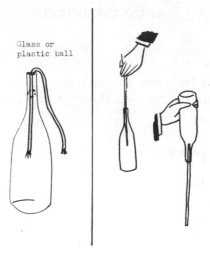

**Figure 26.**

out for examination. Meanwhile, the glass ball is allowed to roll into the awaiting fingertips of the right hand, where it can be secretly pocketed at convenience. The bottle can now be passed for inspection.

## A PINCH OF SALT

From a newspaper, a quantity of silk handkerchiefs are magically produced, these being extracted from holes punctured at various points.

Between each production, a saltshaker mysteriously appears in the hand and finally vanishes, only to reappear through a hole punctured in the newspaper!

### *The Apparatus Required*

A plastic saltshaker.

Remove the base of the shaker so that it becomes an open container.

A number of silk handkerchiefs.

A sheet of newspaper.

With a hot needle, burn two holes on the side of the shaker. Through the holes should be threaded a loop of nylon gut (fisherman's type) (see Fig. 27).

The hollow shaker is filled with silk handkerchiefs.

**Figure 27.**

## The Setup

The shaker, filled with silks, is concealed behind the sheet of newspaper, which rests upon the table.

### Working and Presentation

In picking up the sheet of paper from the table, the second finger of the right hand enters the gut loop, allowing the shaker to be concealed behind the back of the hand and well out of view at this stage.

The left hand assists in showing the newspaper sheet on both sides, while the right remains empty, with the shaker behind (see Fig. 28).

The sheet of paper is brought up in front of the right hand, and the fingers commence in puncturing holes at various points. First, a hole is punctured in the left-hand corner, toward the top of the paper, and the right hand, containing the shaker and now behind, pivots this inward so that its open end is up against the hole. The first silk handkerchief is pulled from the shaker, through the hole, and left to hang on both sides. During the routine the newspaper is constantly shown on both sides, while the right hand remains open, appearing to be empty.

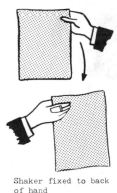

Shaker fixed to back
of hand

**Figure 28.**

133

In fact, several such holes are punctured over the surface of the newspaper, and, simultaneously, silks are produced from these.

To add novelty, and to possibly take advantage of the fact that the shaker can be used for a further magical use, the right hand reaches into the air and produces it by a pivoting movement. The fingers of the right hand simply curl inward for the saltshaker to appear. Imaginary salt is shaken over the newspaper between each production, and by exerting the fingers so that they open fully, the performer can make it vanish.

When all the silks have been produced and emptied from the hollow shaker, this in fact is produced from the newspaper. In puncturing a hole in the central position of the paper, the fingers curl inward so that the shaker can be gripped through. It is, therefore, an easy matter for the performer to disengage the shaker from the second finger and then produce it from the hole punctured in the newspaper.

## MILKY FLIGHT

Here the performer can vanish a half-pint tumbler containing real milk.

From a waxed milk container, milk is poured into a tumbler, which is then covered by an opaque cloth. Throwing the cloth into the air, the glass of milk is seen to completely vanish!

### The Apparatus Required

A disposable waxed milk carton. This should contain enough milk to fill a half-pint glass.

A half-pint tumbler.

A cloth, measuring 24" square. A cardboard disk, the same diameter as the mouth of the tumbler, is sewn to the center of the cloth (see Fig. 29).

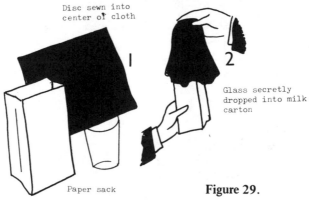

Disc sewn into center of cloth

Glass secretly dropped into milk carton

Paper sack

**Figure 29.**

## The Setup

The carton of milk, tumbler, and cloth are nearby.

## Working and Presentation

Both the carton and tumbler are removed from the table. From the carton, milk is poured into the tumbler. The carton is then placed upon the table with its top *fully* opened.

The cloth is draped over the tumbler so that the disk falls parallel with its mouth.

The gesture that follows should appear to the audience as though the performer wishes to catch any possible overflow of liquid, through bad pouring, into the container.

The waxed container, held in the left hand, is brought up beneath the tumbler for this supposed purpose. In fact, what really happens, is that the entire glass, containing milk, is slowly allowed to slide inside same (see Fig. 29).

However, because of the secret cardboard disc within the handkerchief, the right hand still appears to hold the glass.

The waxed carton, now containing and concealing the tumbler of milk, is placed to one side.

Gripping what appears to be the glass of milk through the material of the cloth, the performer swiftly throws the cloth into the air, where it falls to the floor.

The glass, containing milk, has completely vanished!

Here are some suggested patter lines.

"They tell us all to drink more milk each day, so here is one trick that uses milk alone. Talking about milk, I was amused the other day to learn of the little boy who, after wandering into a field, stumbled across a number of empty milk bottles. 'Is this a cow's nest,' he enquired. Well, what more could I possible say except that tonight I do not use a bottle, for a waxed carton will just have to do. Let's fill the tumbler!

[The tumbler of milk is passed several times in front of the eyes.]

"Well, at least it is 'past-eur-ized [Past your eyes, a corny yet funny remark, one that has to be worded carefully to bring about rewarding results].

"Enough of this, let's cover the tumbler with the handkerchief. This particular trick was invented by the famous Chinese magician Hung Wun, his brother was Hung Two [hung, too], and after cracking a gag like that, I should be hung as well!

"Ladies and gentlemen . . . a tumbler containing milk lies beneath this cloth . . . and in seconds will . . . [throw cloth into the air] . . . vanish from sight. They often say milk is a soft drink . . . but this is ridiculous!"

## CANDLE-SATION

A red colored candle, covered by a white handkerchief, changes so that it appears to be white. The white candle is then lighted, the flame blown out, and then it is wrapped inside a piece of newspaper. Crumpled between the hands, the candle vanishes from inside the paper and in its place is a red silk handkerchief.

### The Apparatus Required

Two faked candles are used to accomplish this startling effect. Made from stout art paper, red and white respectively, these are formed into tubes, into which are fixed genuine candle tops.

The red candle should be made so that it slides over the inner white one. Inside the hollow white candle is a red silk handkerchief.

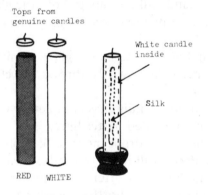

Figure 30.

### The Setup

Place the red candle over the white one, which contains the silk handkerchief. Both candles, appearing as one, should be displayed in a candlestick for both decorative and practical reasons.

A red colored silk handkerchief should be nearby. A box of matches or lighter is also required.

### Working and Presentation

The red candle is removed from the candlestick with the white one containing the silk, as one. It is covered by the white silk handkerchief. A few magical passes are made with the right hand, the same then removing the draped silk together with the outer red shell candle, crumpling this within the folds to prove that it has vanished. The candle being made of paper, it is an easy matter to dispose of the unwanted shell.

Vanished it has, but in its place is a white candle, providing a neat transformation effect.

The performer holds candle in the left hand, and the right hand operates a lighter, lighting the candle, thus proving without a doubt that it must be genuine. The performer extinguishes the flame, and the candle is rolled inside a piece of newspaper, only to be crushed between the hands, leaving the red silk handkerchief inside, this being produced.

## LONG STRETCH

Here is a lesson on how to stretch a piece of rope so that it appears to be ten times its length.

### The Apparatus Required

A stiff paper sack.

A ten-foot length of rope. Sewn onto one end is a snap fastener.

A one-foot length of rope with the other part of the fastener sewn to one end, this coinciding with the one attached to the lengthier rope.

The paper sack is faked, this containing an additional bottom. It consists of a separate piece taken from another similar bag, taped along

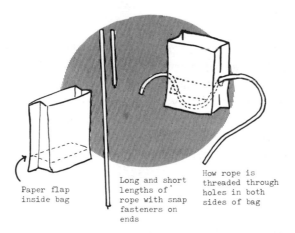

Paper flap
inside bag

Long and short
lengths of
rope with snap
fasteners on
ends

How rope is
threaded through
holes in both
sides of bag

**Figure 31.**

137

one side to form a pivoting flap. Beneath this flap is secreted the ten-foot length of rope with both ends easily accessible, these being positioned on top.

## Working and Presentation

The paper sack is opened and shown to appear empty, while the false bottom cleverly conceals the rope. Rested upright upon the table, the visible one-foot length of rope is seen to be threaded through holes that are punctured in both sides of the sack. But in doing this, the performer secretly lifts up the flap, attaches both snaps so that the rope becomes joined, and brings out the end of the lengthier rope so that it protrudes from the opposite hole.

In pulling each visible end, the rope is seen to emerge longer and longer, until it becomes ten times its original length.

The entire length can be removed from the holes and the paper sack can once again be shown to be empty.


## DICEY MAGIC

The old classic trick "Die through Hat" is known to magicians throughout the world as being a superb effect using a somewhat simple yet convincing principle. It is this principle that we now use for complication of this following effect. Although differing from the "Die through Hat" routine, the same principle, updated, brings about a new and novel presentation.


## The Effect

A cardboard cover is placed over a large die. Six small dice are displayed inside the tray of a common match box. Shaken inside the match box, which is then opened, these are allowed to drop onto the table. However, only four actually fall, leaving two inside, both showing fours on their tops. With four being the prominent number now, the cover is removed from the large die to reveal that all sides but one are bare. The only spotted side happens to depict four spots.


## The Apparatus Required

The special outfit consists of the following:

A solid wooden die measuring three inches square. This should be either painted black or covered in a glossy black paper. Only one of its sides should be spotted, this being the four.

A "Shell" die. Made of stout card, this hollow covering, designed like a genuine die showing spots on all sides, fits over the solid one.

A decorative cover. Made slightly larger than both the solid and shell dice, the interior should be black. The cover fits over the shell, and its outside surface can display a decorative design if wished.

The special matchbox. Of the six dice, two are actually fastened, either by glue or wax, to the base of the inner tray of the matchbox, the remaining four being loose. In sticking both dice onto the inner base of the tray the four-spot sides are made to appear uppermost.

### The Setup

The solid die, displaying one side as a four spot, is set upon the table. Over it is placed the shell. The decorative cover is nearby. The matchbox, containing all six dice, is in the jacket pocket.

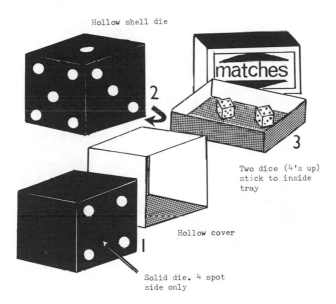

Hollow shell die

matches

Two dice (4's up)
stick to inside
tray

Hollow cover

Solid die. 4 spot
side only

**Figure 32.**

### Working and Presentation

The die is shown to the audience as appearing genuine and covered. The match box is opened, revealing six dice, closed and shaken.

Opened slightly, the box is inverted, allowing only four of the dice to drop onto the table.

"Indeed a strange effect, ladies and gentlemen, for four seems to be the chosen number so far, with four out of the six having actually reacted correctly. Let us close the empty box."

The inner tray is closed, and a pretense is made by the performer, who invisibly catches two imaginary dice from the air, throwing these toward the match box. When the box is opened, both dice have "reappeared," showing four spots on their uppermost sides.

"Strange, did I say . . . and again four is the mystic number."

When the outer cover is lifted from the die, the shell is taken with it, revealing the solid one, which is spotted on one side only. The spots appear to have left five of its sides, for only the four spot remains.

It is one of those "diabolically" clever mysteries!


## SMOKER'S DREAM COME TRUE

First a pipe is produced in the hand, then a cigar, and finally a cigarette and match materialize!

### *The Apparatus Required*

A pipe.
An imitation hollow cigar (joke/novelty type).
A cigarette and match.
An elastic band.
A piece of stout card.

Hollow plastic cigar slides over pipe-stem

**Figure 33.**

### *The Setup*

Cut the end off the plastic cigar. Force the stem of the pipe inside this hollowed fake and attach a small elastic band around both. Push the base of the match stick down through the center of the cigarette, securing this unit alongside the length of the cigar, by the aid of the elastic band (see Fig. 33).

Prior to presentation, the set is held in the hand as shown in Figure 33, the middle finger pivoting the pipe back against the sleeve.

A piece of stout paper should be lying upon the table.

## *Presentation*

The piece of paper is lifted by the left hand (still retaining hold of the unit, as previously described) and then rolled into a tube. In forming the tube, both finger and thumb of the right hand (Fig. 33) pivot the "pipe unit" into the inside the paper, while a continuation of the rolling proceeds. In fact, the pipe unit is now inside the paper roll. An elastic band or plastic bangle, placed over this, enables the tube to stay secure during the performance.

The performer reaches inside one end of the tube and produces, first, the cigar, pulling this away from the stem of the pipe and the elastic band, which holds it in position. Then the cigarette is produced, and while the performer places is aside, the protruding match is gripped between the crutch of the thumb so that it is secretly concealed.

Finally, the performer reaches into the tube and produces the pipe. Placing it between his teeth, he further reaches into the air and produces the match (from the concealed position), striking it, and finally smoking the pipe. A small amount of tobacco can be tightly packed into the bowl, allowing the performer to actually light it when required.

Finally, the paper roll is dropped open and shown to be empty—a smoker's dream come true!

Pipe is pivoted inwards
inside the paper

**Figure 34.**

## COLOR-CHANGING, STRETCHING WAND

We magicians have seen magic wands that rise within the clenched fist, break apart when someone touches them, float in the air, vanish, or change color completely. This new addition to the range of magic wands offers novelty in effect.

The wand, black with white tips, is barely six inches long. Held between the fingers of both hands, it appears to stretch in a most uncanny fashion. As it gets longer, it appears to change its color! The wand is actually stretched to a length of two feet and ends in being that of a red colored one.

The extended wand can be handed out to any member of the audience for thorough examination.

### The Apparatus Required

A two-foot magic wand, made from dowel and painted red with white tips.

A special gimmick in the form of a metal or cardboard tube, measuring three inches, showing a white tip with a portion of black.

This gimmick is slid over the wand to the point where it resembles a small black and white wand, toward one end.

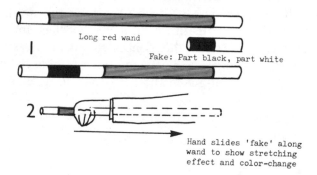

**Figure 35.**

### The Setup

Since this trick is designed as an opener, the conjurer has adequate time in preparing the wand so that it appears to be that of the miniature, black, with two white tips. The majority of the red wand is actually hidden within the right sleeve of the jacket. The right hand holds the remaining portion, which appears to be a small, yet regular, wand (see Fig. 35).

### Working and Presentation

The wand is displayed in the right hand. The fingers of the left assist in stretching it, by holding the opposite end. The right hand now covers the black portion of the sliding tube. Part or most of the white tip attached to this should be clearly visible at this stage. By sliding this tube along the wand, and allowing the audience to see the white tip moving, the stretching illusion is created. However, the wand is seen to have changed its color, for when it has been finally stretched, it is now red with white tips. The sliding tube is secretly retained in the left hand. The stretched wand can now be handed out to a member of the audience.

# Appendix: Major International Magical Societies

To list every magical society and organization in the world would not only be a laborious task, but would involve a complete directory on its own. Such directories are available from various sources and can be obtained through mail-order suppliers.

My intention here is to list only a few, those being the major societies whose purpose it is to provide their members with entertaining talks and lectures, conventions, competitions, and a brotherhood. The student, upon being accepted as a member of any of the societies I list, will share the secrets of his fellow colleagues, and form an important part of such an exclusive society.

The most famous of these societies is The Magic Circle, which has its headquarters in London and meets every Monday night. The clubroom is open to members only, although some open nights are planned during the course of each year's syllabus.

The Magic Circle is privileged to have its own permanent theater, from where many BBC television programs have been repeatedly televised and shown. The museum and library are available to members wishing to delve into both past and present.

The Magic Circle: permanent clubroom, theater, museum, and library at 84, Cheines Mews, London W.C.1., England.

The International Brotherhood of Magicians (Kenton, Ohio):

Headquarters of the famous brotherhood society in which

Mary T. Dowd is executive secretary.

The International Brotherhood of Magicians is divided into "rings," and their magazine, *The Linking Ring,* is for private circulation only, published monthly. Of all the "rings," The British Ring, number 25, is the largest. Secretary and past international president, William G. Stickland, The Wand, Ferndown, Dorset, England, has been an active member and official since its formation.

# A Glossary of Conjuring Terms

ACQUITMENT: Series of moves involved in a sleight, usually to make something vanish or appear, or to keep it concealed.

ACT: The complete rehearsed program as presented.

ASSEMBLY: A card trick in which several cards of a kind are brought together, e.g., the four aces, or all cards of a suit.

BACK-PALM: To conceal an object at the back of the hand.

BIGHT: A loop of rope, string, etc., contained in a knot.

BILL TUBE: A sealed tube in which a bank note or bill, or written message is made to reappear.

BILLET: Small slip of paper on which something is written or drawn.

BISEAUTE: Adjective applied to cards that are narrower at one end than the other. *See also,* Strippers

BLACK ART PRINCIPLE: The principle that black upon black shows no join, or that black upon black is invisible when bright lights are directed toward the spectators.

BLACK LIGHT: Fluorescent lighting, invisible until it falls upon a specially treated surface. By its use, treated objects can be seen through in complete darkness.

BLENDO: A trick using two or more silk squares that magically become one larger square, blending the colors of the smaller silks. E.G., red, white, and blue small squares become a Stars and Stripes, or Union Jack.

BLIND SHUFFLE: Gamblers' term for a shuffle that retains the cards in the original order. In conjurers' parlance, this is more often called a *false shuffle. See also* false shuffle

BOOK TEST: Demonstration in mentalism, in which the performer divines, or predicts, a freely chosen passage in a book or magazine handled by a spectator.

BOTTOM CARD: The card on the face of the pack; the card whose face can be seen when the pack is assembled. The *face card*.

BOTTOM DEAL: The dealing of the bottom card of the pack, secretly, instead of the top card.

BOTTOM STOCK: That portion of a pack of cards which is at the bottom.

BOXING THE CARDS: To cause cards to face each other in the pack.

BREAK: A small gap held at the edge of a pack of cards, and maintained (usually) by the tip of a finger.

BRIDGE: A gap in the pack of cards, caused by bending some cards.

C. AND R.: Abbreviation for Cut and Restored, usually applied to tricks in which a rope, string, thread, or tape is cut and finally mended.

CHANGING BAG: A bag with two (or more) compartments, used for exchanging one article for another.

CHARLIER SYSTEM: An old system of marking cards, originally by pricking small holes in them at specified places. Named after its originator, a nineteenth-century magician and inventor.

CLIPBOARD: A thin board with writing paper clipped to it. There are a number of faked clipboards, by the use of which the magician can detect what has been written on a piece of paper that has been torn off the board. Not used as often as one might suspect.

CONJURER'S CHOICE: No choice at all. *See also* Force

CRIMP: To bend one corner of a card secretly.

CULL: To extract, or assemble together, a number of cards secretly.

CUPS AND BALLS: Centuries-old trick in which balls appear under, and disappear from, three metal cups. Requires considerable skill if it is to be entertaining, because the spectators know what to expect, and the only mystery is not "What's going to happen?" but "How does he do it?" Many modern performers prefer a version using only one cup, known as *chop cup*.

CUT: To divide the pack into two or more sections. A *complete cut* is made when the sections are reassembled.

DAUB: A paste, once popular, for marking cards on the backs or faces.

DECK: American (and old English) term for a pack of cards.

DIACHYLON: A chemical substance used for making one card stick to another and yet be easily separated. *See also* Melrose

DITCH: Slang term meaning "To get rid of something."

DOUBLE-BACKER: Special playing card, printed with a back on each side.

DOUBLE-FACER: Special playing card, printed with a face on each side.

DOUBLE LIFT: To lift two cards so that they appear as one.

DOVETAIL: To shuffle cards by interlacing them. A number of modern card tricks depend upon this being done with one hundred percent accuracy. Very considerable skill is required.

DRAPE: The overhang of a table cover, or the cover itself.

DROP: To drop the balance of cards held in the hand during the shuffle so that they fall upon the shuffled cards.

EFFECT: Description of a trick as seen by the audience. Too often used by conjurers when they mean to say *trick*.

EGG BAG: A trick in which an egg or other small object appears in and disappears from a cloth bag. Much favored by some magicians.

EIGHT KINGS SETUP: An easily memorized prearrangement of a pack of cards, taking its name from the mnemonic "Eight Kings Threaten To Save Nine Fine Ladies For One Sick Knave."

END GRIP: Manner of holding a pack of cards with thumb at one end and fingers at the other.

ESCAPOLOGY: The art and craft of the magician who specializes in escaping from handcuffs, ropes, and other restraints. The term did not exist in Houdini's day, but was coined by an equally skillful performer, Murray, after Houdini's death in 1926.

E.S.P.: Abbreviation for extra-sensory perception, a term invented by Dr. J. B. Rhine, of Duke University, North Carolina, to describe mind reading, clairvoyance, and kindred phenomena achieved by unrecognized physical means. Most conjurers seem to disbelieve all demonstrations of such phenomena. Others are more open-minded. A few are convinced that E.S.P. exists and is practical.

E.S.P. CARDS: Specially designed cards devised by Dr. J. B. Rhine for E.S.P. experiments (*see* E.S.P.). There are five designs: circle, cross, wavy lines, square, and star. A pack of twenty-five E.S.P. cards contains five of each design. Apart from genuine E.S.P. experiments, they are now widely used by conjurers.

FACE CARD: *See* Bottom card.

FAIR SHUFFLE: A genuine shuffle of the cards, as compared to *false shuffle*.

FAKE: Familiar enough as the verb meaning "To make plausible so as to deceive." But conjurers use it more as a noun. A fake is a piece of apparatus, seemingly unprepared but that has been secretly prepared for trickery. *See also* Gimmick

FALSE COUNT: Method of counting cards, coins, etc., so as to show them totaling more or less than their real number.

FALSE SHUFFLE: Method of apparently shuffling a pack of cards without changing their order.

FAN: To manipulate playing cards into the form of a fan.

FANNING POWDER: A chemical powder (zinc stearate) used for making cards smooth and easily manipulated. *See also* Slick card; Zinc stearate

FIND THE LADY: *See* Three-card trick

FINGER-FLINGERS: A class of magicians who delight in showing their ability to perform complicated manipulations, rather than their skill as entertainers. There are very many of them.

FIRST CARD: The top card of the pack when the cards are held face down. Or the first card to be dealt, whether face up or face down.

FLASH PAPER: Tissue paper treated with explosive chemicals so that it will ignite with a brilliant flash when touched with something hot, such as a cigarette end or a match that has just been extinguished.

FLASH WOOL: Cotton wool prepared as is *flash paper.* Highly dangerous, because it can be self-igniting under pressure.

FORCE: To restrict a spectator's choice to a single item, when he believes he has a choice of more than one.

FRENCH DROP: *See* Tourniquet

FOUR ACE TRICK: An *assembly* of the four aces apparently by magical means. There are many versions of this trick, some of which involve dealing cards out and counting them several times.

GHOST TUBE: A tube that can be shown apparently empty, while yet holding goods to be produced later.

GIMMICK: A secret piece of apparatus that is largely responsible for the success of a trick. Used as a verb, it has much the same meaning as *fake.*

GLIDE: To hold back the bottom card and deal the next card to it from under the pack. A kind of *second deal* in reverse, with the dirty work being covered by the pack itself.

HEADLINE PREDICTION: A demonstration of mentalism, in which the performer predicts the headline of a newspaper not yet published. The prediction is often left in a sealed envelope with a member of the audience before the performance and before the paper is published. This calls not only for skill, but for great faith in human nature.

HINDU SHUFFLE: A method of shuffling cards, in which the pack is held on the long sides by each hand, one hand drawing out a batch of cards and replacing them on the rest of the pack.

HOLDOUT: A secret device for containing such things as playing cards so that they are hidden and yet at the immediate disposal of the magician when required. A holdout sometimes extracts cards from the pack and retains them until they are wanted.

HOMING: The magical return of an object, such as a card, coin, ball, etc., to its original place after it has been removed therefrom.

INDIFFERENT CARD: A card other than that with which the trick is being performed. Any card not being used.

INJOG: To replace a card on or in the pack so that its end projects toward the manipulator.

JOG: To replace a card with one end or side projecting slightly.

JUMBO CARDS: Large-sized cards, four times the normal size, used for many card tricks. Very useful for nearsighted spectators in the audience.

KEY CARD: A card in some way distinctive so that it can be recognized by the magician, e.g., by markings, *crimp, glimpse,* etc. *See also* Locator

KNIFE FORCE: Method of forcing a card on a spectator by having him thrust a table knife into the pack. Manipulation then brings the forced card into position above or below the knife blade.

LEVITATION: The raising of an object or a person into the air without any visible means of support. Not to be confused with *suspension.*

LOAD: An article or collection of articles prepared so that it can be secretly inserted into a container for production later, e.g., the rabbit that will appear from a hat. Also, *load* applied to smaller items, such as a thimble, concealed about the person, and discovered apparently by surprise, later in the trick.

LOCATOR: A card specially prepared in some secret way, which can be used for locating other cards in the pack. A locator card can be thick, thin, long, short, or otherwise peculiar so that it is easily distinguished from its fellows.

LONG CARD: A playing card slightly longer than the rest of the pack, used as a *locator.* Also, a joke card that is several times longer than a normal card, and on which the pips are printed in a long, straight line.

MASKING PRINCIPLE: The theory of covering an article with something that matches its background so as to conceal it. E.G., a playing card with newspaper pasted on its back would not be seen if it were laid face down on an open newspaper. Nature does it with birds' eggs!

MECHANICS' GRIP: Believed to be the card sharper's way of holding cards when dealing. The highly unnatural appearance of the hand, though, would make it rather obvious, except in a home for arthritic patients.

MELROSE: Proprietary name for a skin-soothing paste. Its use in magic is confined to making two cards stick together as one, and yet come apart easily when required. An efficient but not so sanitary substitute is saliva. *See also Diachylon.*

MEXICAN TURNOVER: The turning of a *tabled card* with another card, in the course of which the two cards change places. Not to be confused with a Chili con carne pasty.

MENTALISM: The branch of conjuring involving alleged mind reading, clairvoyance, divination, etc., but using practical and physical means to achieve what appears to be psychic results.

MISDIRECTION: The art of misleading the spectator's attention at the critical moment of a trick, e.g., to flourish an empty hand in which something is believed to be concealed, while secretly disposing of the article with the other hand. Practice is needed by the novice, to avoid blinking or screwing up the eyes at the moment of misdirection.

MOVE: The manipulation required to perform a trick.

ONE-AHEAD: A useful bit of psychological skullduggery by which the *mentalist,* by learning the identity of one object, is able to divine the names of others and to reveal them, in the wrong order but correctly.

ONE-WAY PACK: A pack of cards with an asymmetrical design on the back so that one end differs from the other. The difference might be considerable (e.g., a picture of a flower—flower at one end, stalk at the other) or very slight indeed, such as a minute printing imperfection in an otherwise symmetrical pattern. The American Angel back Bicycle brand is an example of the latter.

OUTJOG: To replace a card on or in the pack so that its end projects away from the manipulator.

OVERHAND SHUFFLE: The normal way of shuffling cards in Britain, in which the cards, held edgeways in the left hand, are picked up and replaced in batches by the right hand. (All right, the other way round if you are left-handed.)

PACK: In the United States and Britain the normal pack of cards has fifty-two cards, with two jokers (sometimes three) and one or two blanks. Some Continental packs number only thirty-two cards, plus joker(s).

PALM: To conceal an object secretly in the hand, not necessarily by a convulsive clutch in the actual palm. The Finger Palm, in which the object is resting on the curled fingers of the otherwise empty hand, is favored by skilled magicians, and presents a more natural appearance of the hand.

PASS: A pass used to be the description of a gesture accompanied by a magic word ("Hey Presto . . . Pass!"). Today it usually means the secret exchanging of positions of two halves of a pack of cards. In the United States this is sometimes known as "Jumping the cut."

PASS OFF: To convey away, secretly, some article that is carried off-stage by an assistant or a mechanical device.

PEEK: A *Glimpse* to sight a card or other object quickly and secretly.

PREARRANGEMENT: The arrangement beforehand of articles such as a pack of cards in some recognizable order, though this should not be apparent to the spectator. *See also* Eight Kings Setup

PREDICTION: In which the *mentalist* forecasts some future event, such as the card somebody will choose, the thought he will have, the

151

word he will write, etc. The mentalist featuring a prediction should be prepared to answer the question "If you can do this sort of thing, why don't you get rich by predicting racing winners, political results, rising stocks and shares, etc.!" There *are* suitable answers, when you come to think about it.

PRODUCTION: Quite apart from its theatrical connotation, this is used to mean just what it says: the production of articles from a supposedly empty container, or from "thin air." In many illusions, living people and livestock are so produced.

PRINCIPLE: The method by which a particular trick, or series of tricks, is performed.

PROPS: Short for "properties": the apparatus, seen and unseen, required for performance of a trick. Also, such items as tables, stands, etc., are props. It is a general theatrical term and applies to all the materials, apart from costumes and scenery, used in stage productions.

READERS: Playing cards marked on the backs so that the magician can "read" their values without seeing their faces. Not nearly so frequently used as many people suspect.

RECOVERY: The resumption of control of an article used in magic, such as the regaining of a billiard ball secretly and temporarily placed beneath the arm.

RESET: To prepare afresh a piece of apparatus requiring preparation each time it is used, e.g., to wind up a secret piece of clockwork before performance, or to adjust a secret trapdoor so that it is ready for use.

REVERSED CARD: A playing card that is returned to the pack either back to front or upside down. *See* One-way Pack

RIBBON SPREAD: To lay out the cards in a line or arc by a single sweep of the hand.

RIFFLE: To thumb the ends of the cards so that each card falls rapidly after the preceding one. The Riffle Shuffle is performed in this manner. *See* Dovetail

ROPE CEMENT: An adhesive, sometimes used for joining two pieces of rope.

ROUGHING FLUID: A chemical substance that, applied to cards, roughens their surface and makes them slightly tacky. Can be made at home by mixing Canada balsam and carbon tetrachloride.

ROUTINE: The showmanlike arrangement of each trick. Also, the planning of a series of tricks so that they blend naturally.

RUN: To slide off one card at a time in a shuffle.

SECOND DEAL: To deal the second card from the top of the pack instead of the first card. This requires great skill and constant practice to perform adequately, and few magicians can do a good second deal.

SET: To prepare a piece of apparatus ready for the conjurer's performance. *See also* Reset

SETUP: The prearrangement of apparatus, usually playing cards, so that it follows a certain sequence. Also applies to certain mathematical tricks.

SERVANTE: A hidden shelf or suspended pocket, behind the table or chair or otherwise concealed, to receive items discarded or exchanged. Much in vogue among Victorian magicians, who made great with their elaborate stage furniture, most of which was riddled with traps and wells and festooned with shelves and hooks.

SHIFT: Another name for the *pass* with cards.

SHORT CARD: A playing card that is shorter than the rest of the pack.

SHUFFLE: To mix the cards.

SHUFFLE OFF: To conclude a false shuffle by genuinely shuffling the balance of the pack.

SIDE-GRIP: The practice of holding a pack of cards by its long edges.

SI STEBBINS SETUP: A pack setup in a certain numerical sequence, whereby the magician can tell the position of every card in the pack.

SIGHT: *See* Glimpse; Peek

SLEEVE (to): To insert secretly an article in the sleeve. This principle is not nearly so often used as popular fancy believes. But when it *is* used, the skilled magician makes it completely imperceptible and deceiving. A good sleeve worker has the uncanny skill of the juggler, and the precision of a marksman.

SLEIGHT: The secret manipulation required to perform a trick. This could be extremely simple, such as pretending to drop a coin and retaining it in the *Finger Palm,* or it could be fantastically difficult, like some of the modern card sleights.

SLICK CARD: A card that is highly polished (car polish) so that it slides more easily than the rest of the pack. Today, *fanning powder* does the job equally well.

SLIP: A card sleight in which the top card of the pack is imperceptibly slipped onto the lower half of the pack when the cards are cut.

SPIRIT LOCK: A specially prepared padlock that springs open on the word of command, or after a set time.

SQUARE: To adjust the edges of a pack of cards by pressing them into alignment with fingers and thumb after the cards have been, say, shuffled. Many sleights can be performed in the act of squaring up the pack.

STACK: A prearranged pack of cards. *See also* Setup

STAGE MONEY: Imitation bank notes and treasury bills, used for stage purposes, including conjuring.

STEAL: Not used in its dishonest connotation in magic, where the word merely means to abstact an article secretly, e.g., to palm a card off the surface of the pack while handing it (the pack) out for examination. Also generally used in terms of securing the *load,* as in the case of the Multiplying Billiard Balls.

STEAMBOATS: A particular kind of thin, flexible playing cards with a plaid design on the back, particularly favored by card manipulators at one time. Popularly believed to be so called because they were cheap, expendable cards used by gamblers on the Mississippi steamboats. The term is also sometimes used to describe playing cards having an all-over back design (geometrical) without white borders.

STOCK: The main portion of a pack of cards, as opposed to those being immediately dealt or otherwise used for playing or magical purposes.

STOOGE: A secret confederate among the spectators, or one who has been primed to say or do a certain thing, without necessarily knowing why he must do so.

STRIPPERS: Playing cards that are wider at one end than at the other. *See also* Biseaute

SWAMI GIMMICK: A secret writing aid used by mentalists.

SWITCH: To exchange one article for another imperceptibly and secretly.

SUSPENSION: To maintain an object or person in midair, without apparent support, or by means of a physically impossible support, such as a sword point under the elbow. Not to be confused with *levitation.*

TABLED CARD: The card on the table, as opposed to those in the hand.

TALKING: Noise made by secret apparatus when in use, always undesirable, because it betrays the secret that some unseen piece of equipment is being employed. E.g., an unseen spring, when released, might emit a loud clank.

THREE-CARD TRICK: Or "Find the Lady." A card swindle on which many tricks are based.

THROW: To deposit the balance of the cards upon the rest after a shuffle.

THUMB COUNT: The art of secretly counting cards held in one hand, by letting them slip rapidly across the thumb. Sometimes both hands are used, but this method is not so imperceptible as the one-handed method.

TOP CARD: The card lying face down at the back of the pack, or the card lying face up when the pack is turned over.

TOURNIQUET: Also known as the "French Drop." The act of pretending to take an object in one hand, while it is secretly retained

154

in the other hand. Most convincing when properly executed but a reasonable excuse must be provided to explain (by implication) the need to take the object from one hand to the other.

TRANSPOSITION: The exchange of position between one object and another, e.g., a bottle is placed under the right-hand tube, and a tumbler under the left-hand tube. On lifting the tubes again, the two objects have apparently changed places, bottle to left and tumbler to right tube.

UNDERCUT: To take the lower section of a pack of cards and place it on the upper section.

UPPERCUT: To take the upper section and place it beneath the lower section of the pack.

VANISH: Used as a transitive verb by magicians, as well as being employed as a noun. Simply means to make something disappear, or its disappearance.

WAND: The original source of the magician's wonders in the good old days but now sadly debased in importance by those who use it in a comedy fashion. Apart from its actual occult use, the wand in the hand of a conjurer helps him to conceal some small article in the hand, to direct (or misdirect) attention to some part of the stage or audience, to poke things in and out of tubes, to hang things upon, or (all too rarely) to rap some hell-raising child assistant upon the knuckles. For some unknown reason, they are nearly all black, with white tips.

WAX: A sort of soft beeswax in various colors, used by magicians as an adherent or adhesive. Mainly used in card work.

WELL: A secret cavity, usually in the conjurer's table, that is concealed by the *Black Art Principle*. Not used so often these days as it was years ago.

X-RAY EYE ACT: The performance of otherwise normal, as well as remarkable, tasks while thoroughly blindfolded. Kuda Bux, from Kashmir, created a great furor in Britain and the United States with his X-ray Act in the 1940s and 1950s. Since then many fine methods have been invented for performing this astonishing type of act. Nowadays it is used by expert performers who drive cars, fire rifles at living targets, or deliver sealed messages to addresses supposedly unknown to them. A splendid publicity device, and one that invariably attracts large, appreciative audiences.

ZINC STEARATE: A chemical powder used on the feet of athletes originally, but now in great demand by card manipulators to prepare cards so that they slide smoothly and easily. *See also* Fanning Powder.

# Bibliography

Books and periodicals on magic fall into several distinct categories and between them cover all aspects of the art.

General books, obtainable from bookstores and libraries anywhere, are usually written for the beginner or amateur.

Technical books, those of an advanced nature, are not generally available to the public; they contain professional secrets and are obtainable from mail-order specialist publishers.

## BOOKS

Adair, Ian. *Encyclopaedia of Dove Magic.* vols. 1-4. Bideford: Supreme Magic Company Ltd, 1969, 1970, 1973, 1976, 1978. Four volumes containing the real secrets of producing doves from silk handkerchiefs, vanishes, changes, and transpositions.

____. *Magic Step by Step.* New York: Arco Publishing Co., 1972. Original magic designed for the amateur.

____. *The KnowHow Book of Jokes and Tricks.* London: Usborne Publishing, 1977. Designed for the child magician, this is a book containing full-color cartoon illustrations, outlining the basic elements of the craft.

____. *Television Card Manipulations.* Bideford: Supreme Magic Company Ltd, 1962. Magic with emphasis on visual card presentation.

Bobo, J. B. *The New Modern Coin Magic.* Chicago: Magic Inc., 1966. A complete work on the manipulation and techniques as used in coin magic.

Booth, John. *The John Booth Classics.* Bideford: Supreme Magic Company Ltd, 1975. The author's professional magical experiences. New and original magic from a man of great knowledge.

Braue, Fred, and Hugard, Jean. *Expert Card Techniques.* London: Faber & Faber Ltd, 1954. Classic card magic for both beginners and advance performers.

____. *The Royal Road to Card Magic.* London: Faber & Faber Ltd, 1949. A step-by-step course in card conjuring.

Clive, Paul. *Card Tricks Without Skill.* London: Faber & Faber Ltd, 1971. A wide range of card tricks.

Dexter, Will. *Feature Magic for Mentalists.* Bideford: Supreme Magic Company Ltd, 1975. A book containing clever and original brainstorms from the author of many best-selling books on the craft.

Fox, Karrell. *Clever Like a Fox.* Bideford: Supreme Magic Company Ltd, 1976. Clever general effects introducing comedy material.

Ganson, Lewis. *The Art of Close-up Magic.* vols. 1 and 2. Bideford: Supreme Magic Company Ltd, 1970. Brilliant magical close-up items that can be presented surrounded. Both volumes include tricks that solely use household items.

____. *Card Magic by Manipulation.* Bideford: Supreme Magic Company Ltd, 1971. Professional methods of producing, vanishing, and exchanging cards for manipulation.

____. *Cy Enfield's Entertaining Card Magic.* 3 vols. Bideford: Supreme Magic Company Ltd, 1974. Parts 1, 2, and 3 in paperback. Bound edition comprising all three parts. Tricks of a high standard.

____. *Inner Secrets of Card Magic, More Inner Secrets of Card Magic, Further Inner Secrets of Card Magic, Ultimate Secrets of Card Magic.* Bideford: Supreme Magic Company Ltd, 1970. Advanced work.

____. *Magic of the Mind.* Bideford: Supreme Magic Company Ltd, 1970. Stunning mind-reading experiments designed for an adult audience.

Gibson, Walter. *The Complete Illustrated Book of Card Magic.* London: Kaye & Ward Ltd, 1970. A complete work on card magic, from manipulation to the presentation of simple card tricks.

Gill, Robert. *Magic as a Performing Art.* London: Boker Publishing Co., 1976. The first bibliography of books dealing solely with publications published over the period of the last thirty years. Over 1,000 single entries are listed, these available to the student of magic.

Kaye, Marvin. *The Complete Magician.* London: MacMillan & Co. Ltd, 1974. All aspects of conjuring covered, with a large section on card tricks and sleight-of-hand methods.

Lamb, Geoffrey. *Your Book of Card Tricks.* London: Faber & Faber Ltd, 1972. Selected card tricks for the beginner.

McComb, Billy. *McComb's Magic: 25 Years Wiser.* Bideford: Supreme Magic Company Ltd, 1972. A book of practical ideas from a professional.

Pavel. *The Magic of Pavel.* Bideford: Supreme Magic Company Ltd, 1970. Original material from one of magic's most prolific inventors.

Rice, Harold. *Rice's Encyclopedias of Silk Magic.* vols. 1-3. Wynnewood, Silk King Studios, 1962. Classic and original concepts using silk handkerchiefs.

Stickland, William G. *Introducing Bill's Magic.* Bideford: Supreme Magic Company

Ltd, 1970. Unusual effects using new principles. Strictly mechanical devices to produce stunning results.

Wade, John. *The Trade of the Tricks.* London: Elm Tree Books Ltd, 1974. The compilation of anecdotes; the valuable advice on historical times, coupled by interesting information of the Magic Circle, London.


# PERIODICALS

Weekly, monthly, and bimonthly periodicals are produced in several countries and are available on subscription or through a specialist dealer, but not through the normal channels—newsstands and bookstores. General magic is covered, and all include a variety of effects using various branches of the art.

*Abracadabra.* Birmingham: Goodliffe Publications. Published weekly. Novel conjuring effects invented by the leading specialists.

*The Genii.* Edited by William Larsen. Hollywood: Genii Publications. Published monthly. Regular columnists, well-illustrated tricks and effects.

*The Magigram.* Edited by Ken de Courcy. Bideford: Supreme Magic Company Ltd. Published monthly. A large-sized magazine containing countless tricks and routines. Monthly columnists help to make the magazine a leading one in its field.

*The New Pentagram.* Edited by Peter Warlock. Bideford: Supreme Magic Company Ltd. Published monthly. Intriguing, sophisticated effects; famous exponents discuss their presentations.

*The Tops.* Edited by Neil Foster. Colon, Michigan: Abbots Manufacturing Co. Published monthly. Current affairs in the world of magic; plenty of all-around magical effects.

# Index